# Wild Things

## to Sew and Wear

# Acknowledgements

Thank you to the talented editors at Quantum for their leadership throughout the process of creating this book. In particular Hazel Eriksson, who seamlessly adopted the project; Liz Jones who was my dauntless guide in creating and organising the projects and designer Rosamund Saunders who made everything cohesive and beautiful. I feel very lucky to have worked with such a stellar team!

A big thank you to photographer Hoyoung Lee for creating such enduring images from a truly wild photo shoot, and Sojung Lee for styling and helping wrangle kiddos.

I must also thank my original wild thing, Carter, and my husband Wayne, who were patient and always supportive throughout an entire year of mummy getting up very, very early to sew, draw and paint. You are both my inspiration and my motivation!

**Wild Things to Sew and Wear**
Copyright © 2014 Quantum Publishing Ltd

Frances Lincoln Limited
74–77 White Lion Street
London N1 9PF
www.franceslincoln.com

ISBN: 978-0-7112-3601-1

First UK Edition printed August 2014

This book was conceived and produced by
Quantum Publishing
6 Blundell Street
London N7 9BH

QUMWTSW

**Publisher:** Sarah Bloxham
**Project Editor:** Hazel Eriksson
**Editor:** Liz Jones
**Designer:** Rosamund Saunders
**Production Manager:** Rohana Yusof

**Illustrator:** Molly Goodall
**Photographer:** Hoyoung Lee of Sohostory

And special thanks to our wild models Bliss, Carter, Quin, and Tessa

Printed in China by 1010 Printing International Ltd

10 9 8 7 6 5 4 3 2 1

# Wild Things

## to Sew and Wear

MOLLY GOODALL

F

FRANCES LINCOLN LIMITED

PUBLISHERS

# Contents

**Wild Animals**

**Woodland Animals**

**Farm Animals**

Cosy Koala Hat 26

Little Leopard Skirt 30

Elephant Friends Shirt 36

Cute Hoot Owl Hat 58

Foxy Scarf 62

Butterfly Beach Cape 68

Pony Overalls 86

Kitty and Mouse Mittens 92

Buzzy Bee Rain Cape 96

## Sewing Techniques and Patterns

# Foreword

In an era when sewing for children is no longer a necessity, it undoubtedly remains an act of love. When we sew for a little one we put thought into so many details with regard to the child for whom we are creating – style, fit, fabrication, durability and ease of laundering.

In our hearts we hope this thought and planning will translate into a cherished and useful garment. But the garments we create can also have another purpose: the potential to inspire. When I began to sew for my toddler son I started with simple projects, as new mothers do. It felt good to create something and fit it into my mummy schedule of never seeming to have more than 10 or 20 minutes to spare. I annexed my dining room table and created a cutting space at one end, a sewing space at the other, with my ironing board nearby.

While initially fulfilling, soon a problem arose which changed the way I thought about sewing for him. The weather got colder, and my son refused to wear a hat or hood. He had recurring ear infections, so it was imperative that I find a way to keep his head warm while not curtailing the outdoor playtime he cherished. On a trip to a fabric store some bright yellow felt caught my eye and inspiration struck – what if I created a jacket to transform him into a roaring lion? Part costume, part coat, it would keep him warm and encourage him to wear his hood. Many coats later, I am still thrilled at the magical ability creative clothing has to inspire a child, and take the fight out of getting dressed. The new struggle is getting them to take it off for washing!

With this book I offer a variety of ideas to excite both you and your tiny loved ones. I hope you will involve them in the creative process, selecting colours and fabrics, or perhaps adding a special detail to suit their personality. I hope they will take an interest as you work at your machine and marvel at how flat pieces of fabric combine to make a three-dimensional cape or jacket or vest. Most of all, I hope you will spend many joyful hours watching your little wild thing play in your unique creation.

# About This Book

## PROJECT INSTRUCTIONS

### Size and difficulty level

This indicates the size as photographed, and as per the pattern guide at the back of the book. Other sizes are included on the CD.

### You will need box

All the tools and materials you will need to make up the project are listed here.

### Illustrations

Clear step-by-step illustrations complement the instruction text to show you exactly what needs to be done at each stage.

## PATTERN GUIDES

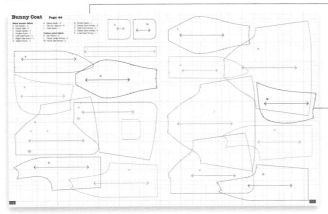

### Key to cutting

This key corresponds to the orange boxes given on the project pages. It will tell you the name of each pattern piece, and guide you in cutting your fabrics.

### Pattern Pieces

Each pattern piece can be identified by a letter which corresponds to the key. Turn to page 111 for a guide to understanding the pattern marks, and to page 103 for information on using the pattern pieces.

## Sizing

Small: 18/24 mo; Medium: 3/4 yrs; Large 5/6 yrs.

| Centimeters | S | | M | | L | |
|---|---|---|---|---|---|---|
| Size | 12m | 2T | 3T | 4T | 5 | 6 |
| Chest | 46–51 | 53 | 56 | 59 | 61 | 64 |
| Height | 79 | 87 | 94 | 102 | 109 | 117 |

| Inches | S | | M | | L | |
|---|---|---|---|---|---|---|
| Size | 12m | 2T | 3T | 4T | 5 | 6 |
| Chest | 18–20 | 21 | 22 | 23 | 24 | 25 |
| Height | 31 | 34 | 37 | 40 | 43 | 46 |

## Before you start

Choose your size, then use the CD to print out all necessary pattern pieces. Cut out all the fabric pieces, using the orange boxes and the pattern guides as references. Make sure you cut on the correct grain line and transfer any marks from the pattern to the fabric. For more information on working with patterns, see pages 103–5 and 111).

All seam allowances are 1.3cm (½in) unless otherwise specified. The fabric amounts will cover the large size, and are given as lengths, assuming a standard width of 115cm (45in).

# Wild Animals

# Roaring Lion Coat

Wouldn't it be more fun to put on your coat if it transformed you into a roaring lion? This charming design will do just that, with its ferocious lion head hood, fierce 'claw'-tipped sleeves, and twitchy tail. Sure to inspire even the wildest little animal to put up their hood in the cold!

## You will need

**Yellow wool felt** – 180cm (2yd) – Cut 2×A, B, 2×C, 2×D, E, 2×F, G, 4×H, 2×I, 2×J, K

**Charmeuse fabric** for sleeve lining – 69cm (¾yd) – Cut 2×P

**Fleece or sherpa** for hood and body lining – 69cm (¾yd) – Cut L, 2×M, N, 2×O

**Contrast cream wool felt** for muzzle and ear fronts – 22cm (¼yd) – Cut 2×A, Q, 2×R, S

**Black wool felt** – 25cm (10in) square scrap – Cut T, 2×U, 6×V

**Thread** to match yellow and black felt and linings

**Thick yarn** for mane and tail – 1 skein

**White felt** for teeth – 7.5cm (3in) square scrap – Cut 2×W

**Buttons** for eyes – 2, 1.5cm (⅝in) in diameter

**Buttons** for front – 4, 2.5cm (1in) in diameter

**Cardboard** for making mane and tail – 15cm by 30cm (6in by 12in) piece

**Tracing paper** for mane and tail assembly – 4 long pieces

**Fabric glue**

**Masking tape**

**See pattern guide on page 112**

With right sides together, sew the centre back seam and press open. If desired, topstitch seam from right side 6mm (¼in) from centre back. Sew lower back to yoke with right sides together; press open. If desired, topstitch. With right sides together, position and sew pocket backs between notches. Press seams open.

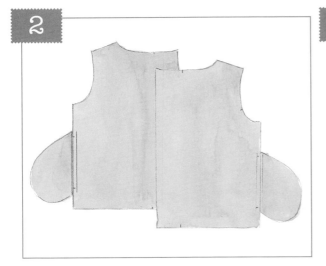

Repeat with pocket fronts and side fronts.

Sew side fronts to side backs at shoulders and side seams, leaving open between notches. Press shoulder seams toward the back and topstitch in place 6mm (¼in) from the seam.

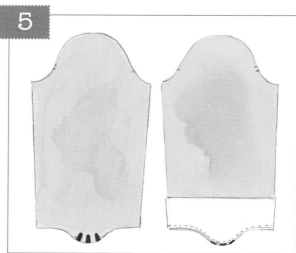

Fold and press pocket fronts and backs to side fronts; pin in place. From wrong side, stitch pocket front and backs to side fronts. This seam will show from the front as decorative topstitching, so take your time and be very neat as you tackle the curves.

With right sides together, position claws at notches on sleeve ends as shown, and baste in place 6mm (¼in) from the edge. With right sides together, place sleeve facing on top of sleeve and claws and sew in place with a 6mm (¼in) seam allowance.

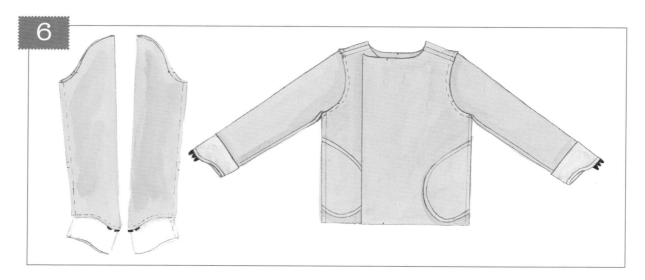

Fold sleeves in half lengthwise (with right sides facing), matching notches. Sew underarm seam from armpit to the end of sleeve facing. Use a sleeve board or rolled towel to press seams open. With right sides together, matching notches and underarm seams, pin sleeves into body of coat. Stitch. Fold sleeve facings to inside, press. Topstitch sleeve ends 1cm (⅜in) from edge. Turn coat body to right side.

**7**

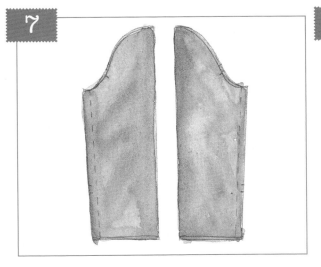

Fold sleeve linings in half lengthwise, matching notches and with right sides together. Sew underarm seams.

**8**

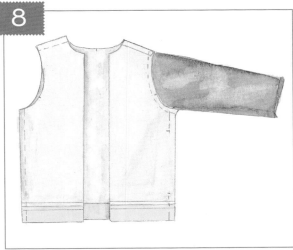

Right sides together, sew back hem facing to lining back. Press open. Repeat for side front hem facings and lining side fronts. Right sides together, sew lining side fronts to lining back at shoulders and side seams, stopping at notches. Right sides together, matching notches and underarm seams, pin sleeve linings into coat lining. Stitch.

**9**

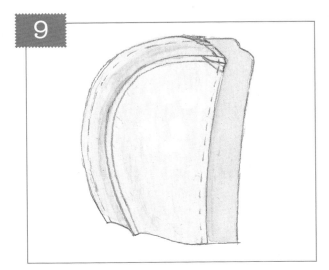

With right sides together, sew hood lining sides to hood lining centre with a 6mm (¼in) seam allowance, matching notches. Press seams open at front edge. With right sides together, sew hood front facing to hood lining with a 6mm (¼in) seam allowance.

### Note
You may need to make the pattern pieces for the hood and body lining slightly smaller if the fleece you choose for them has a lot of stretch. If the fabric is quite firm and a 12.5cm (5in) square will not stretch more than 4cm (1½in) in either direction, cut the lining in your original pattern size and assemble as directed. If it is quite stretchy in both directions, consider cutting the linings a size smaller than your pattern size (if you are sewing a size L, consider cutting the knit linings size M) so that the linings will not sag.

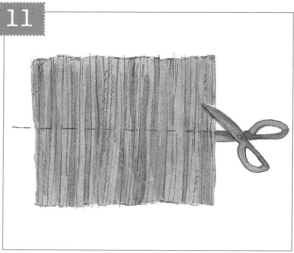

To make the mane and tail, cut a piece of cardboard 15cm (6in) wide and roughly 30cm (12in) long. Wrap yarn for mane and tail around cardboard 200–250 times. Yarn should be about 15mm (⅝in) thick on each side. When yarn is wrapped, use sharp scissors to cut yarn down the middle of the front of the board, releasing it.

Use scissors to cut down centre of yarn again as it lies flat, so that you are left with two rows of 15cm- (6in-) long yarn pieces. Remove small bunch for tail tassel; set aside.

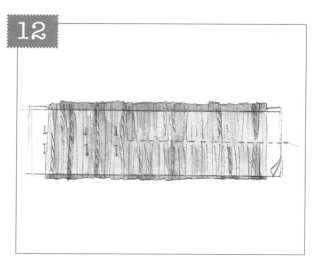

**Note**
Tracing paper or pattern-making paper that comes on a roll works best; this can be purchased from an art supply store—tissue paper will be too thin and liable to tear.

Cut two pieces of tracing paper 60cm (24in) long and about 120cm (48in) wide. Lay one piece on the table and position yarn pieces in one column, with about 2.5cm (1in) of space at top and bottom. Layer second piece of tracing paper on top, and secure all layers with quilting pins. Sew through all layers down the centre.

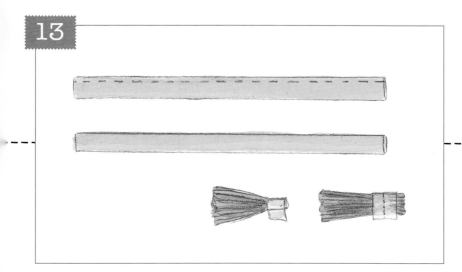

Fold the tail lengthwise with right sides together and stitch a scant 6mm (¼in) from edge. Turn using a loop turner; press. Fold a small swatch of tracing paper around the top edge of the bunch of yarn pieces reserved for the tail tassel. Stitch backward and forward several times through all layers. Gently tear away the paper – the stitching will have created a perforation.

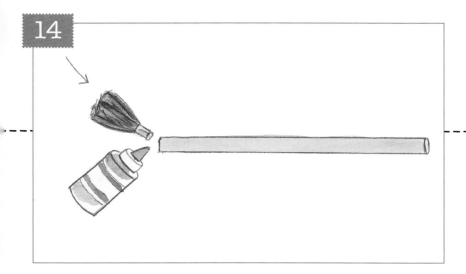

Tightly wrap tip of tassel with a piece of masking tape, covering stitching. Trim end of masking tape off if necessary. Inserting tip of bottle of fabric glue into bottom end of tail, squeeze glue into tail end. Being careful not to close tail end, slide taped part of tail tassel into end of tail. Use a chopstick to gently press tassel farther into the tail end. Set aside to dry. When dry, trim tassel ends straight across.

**15**

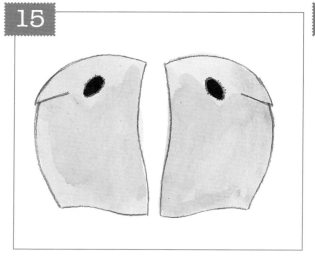

Use a fabric marking pencil to transfer the placement/ stitching lines on the pattern for the mane and fringe to the right side of hood centre and sides. Following guide on pattern, position eyes on right sides of hood sides and secure in place with a dab of glue. Stitch in place using a zigzag or appliqué stitch.

**16**

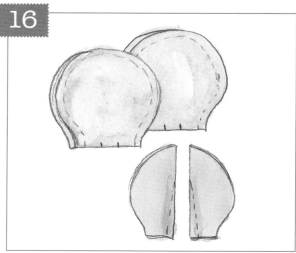

With right sides together, sew ear fronts to ear backs using a 6mm (¼in) seam allowance. Turn and press flat. Fold ears in half as shown, matching notches, and stitch small darts in place through all layers.

**17**

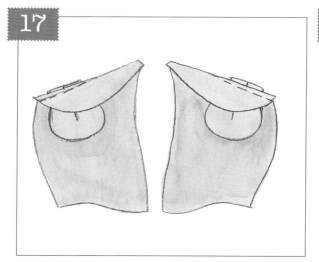

Position ears in slashes on hood sides as shown (front sides of ears to face right side of hood sides), and stitch darts closed to secure ears in place.

**18**

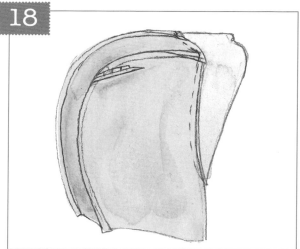

With right sides together, using a 6mm (¼in) seam allowance, sew hood sides to hood centre, matching notches. Press seams open at front and bottom of hood. With right sides together, using a 6 mm (¼in) seam allowance, sew muzzle piece to front of hood. Turn to right side.

**19**

Place nose on hood front in position indicated on patterns; secure in place with a dab of glue. Stitch in place using a zigzag or appliqué stitch. Sew buttons in place on appliquéd felt eyes, securing first with a dab of glue. Position white felt teeth at notches on front of face; baste in place with a 6mm (¼in) seam allowance.

**20**

Measure the line on centre front hood for placement of fringe. Cut a section off of yarn mane to this length (cut through tracing paper and then snip through stitching, pull gently apart from remaining mane). Position stitched seam on fringe along line on centre front hood as above; stitch in place through all thicknesses. This will be time consuming; go slowly and check placement often as you sew.

**21**

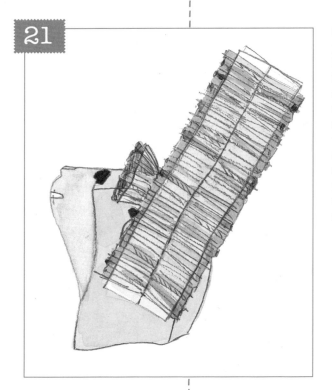

Beginning at end of line on lower left side front hood, position the remaining length of mane with stitching line, matching placement line on hood. Sew mane in place through all thicknesses, going slowly and repositioning the hood often to work it through the machine. This will be even more time consuming; go slowly and check placement often as you sew. Sew all the way across the hood centre and down the other side. If mane runs out, add additional pieces using same method as original. When mane is securely sewn in place, gently tear away all the paper. You may wish to lay the hood flat and trim the lion's mane to the desired length.

**22**

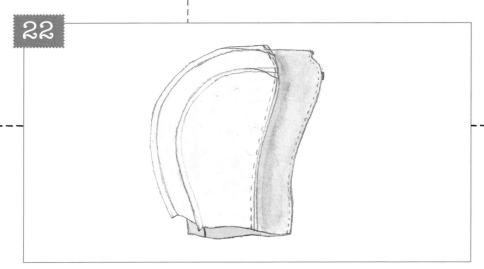

Fit hood into hood lining with right sides together. Stitch together along front edge using a 6mm (¼in) seam allowance, sandwiching teeth between two layers. Turn to right side. Understitch hood facing very close to hood front edge, catching seam allowance in understitching. Baste hood lining to hood at bottom edge, in preparation for setting it into the coat.

**23**

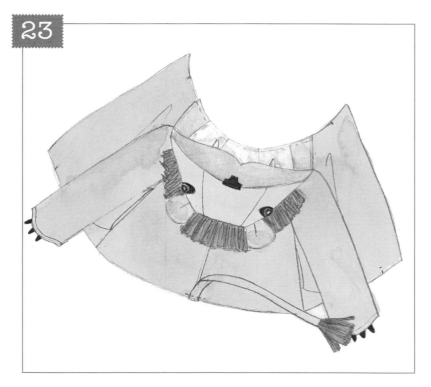

Position hood on coat with right sides together, matching notches, and pin in place. Sew hood to coat with a 1cm (⅜in) seam allowance. Baste tail in position as shown, using a 6mm (¼in) seam allowance. Pin tail upward on coat to keep it out of the way during remaining construction steps. With right sides together, match notches of coat side front edges with lining side front edges; sew together. Fold coat side fronts back on themselves, matching notches, to form facings as shown below. Pin coat to lining along neckline and hemline. Sew neckline and hemline closed.

**24**

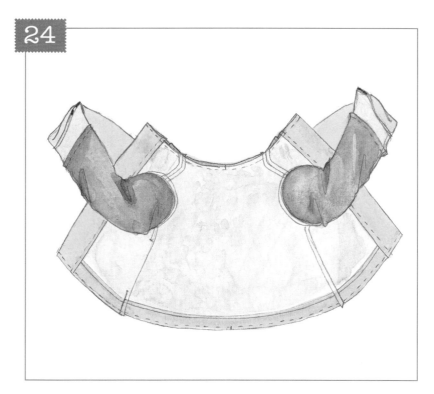

With right sides together, pin ends of sleeve lining to ends of sleeve facings; begin by matching undersleeve seams. Sew together. Carefully turn coat to right side through opening in lining side seam. Hand or machine sew opening in lining closed. Press hem and front edges. Mark buttons and buttonhole placement on front of coat in positions indicated on pattern. Sew buttonholes; sew buttons in place. Your lion is ready to roar and play!

# Bear Hug Vest

A vest with a teddy-bear twist. The adorable faux fur hood and bear-paw pockets are soft and cosy, and it is lined in fleece for warmth. You can experiment with different colours of fur for different bears. This vest was made using a pre-quilted fabric, but it would work equally well with an unquilted wool.

## You will need

**Quilted or woven fabric** for the body – 90cm (1yd) – Cut 2×A, B, C, D

**Faux fur fabric** – 45cm (½yd) – Cut 2×H , 4×K, L, M, 2×N, 2×O

**Fleece fabric** for lining – 90cm (1yd) – Cut F, 2×G, 2×H, 2×I, J

**Black felt** for claws – 25cm (10in) square scrap – Cut 12×E

**Buttons** – 4, 1.5cm (⅝in) in diameter

**Batting** to stuff claws

**Thread** to match

**See pattern guide on page 114**

## A note before sewing

Depending on the depth of pile (length of the hair) of the faux fur you are using, it may be easier to trim the hairs in the seam allowances to reduce bulk. We will use 1cm (⅜in) seam allowances on much of the project to accommodate the fur pile.

**1**

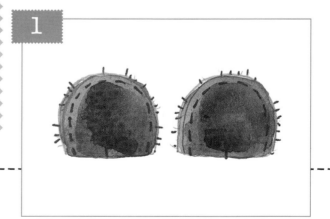

With right sides together, sew the ears using a 1cm (⅜in) seam allowance. Turn to the right side.

**2**

With right sides together, using a 13mm (½in) seam allowance, sew hood sides to hood top centre and hood bottom centre. With right sides together, using a 13mm (½in) seam allowance, sew hood lining sides to hood lining centre, matching notches.

**3**

Position ears on right side of opening in top of hood, as shown. Stitch from centre out to each end, beginning at centre, with a 13mm (½in) seam allowance and tapering to nothing on each side of the hood.

**4**

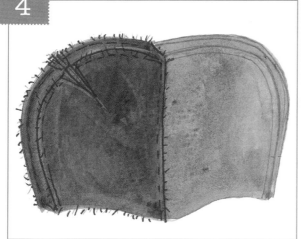

Sew hood lining to hood, with right sides together and matching seams, as shown. Fold hood lining inside hood and baste together at neck seam. The hood is now ready to be set into the vest.

**5**

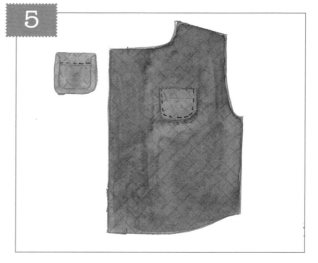

Fold 2.5cm (1in) to wrong side of top edge of pocket; topstitch 2cm (¾in) from edge. Neatly fold 1cm (⅜in) to wrong side all the way around the pocket as shown; press. Position pocket on right side of vest side front as indicated on pattern and topstitch in place a scant 3mm (⅛in) from edge.

**6**

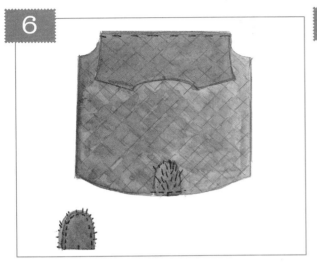

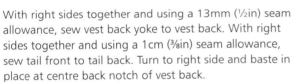

With right sides together and using a 13mm (½in) seam allowance, sew vest back yoke to vest back. With right sides together and using a 1cm (⅜in) seam allowance, sew tail front to tail back. Turn to right side and baste in place at centre back notch of vest back.

**7**

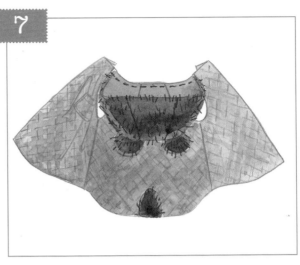

Matching notches, sew hood to vest as shown, using a 1cm (⅜in) seam allowance. Fold front facings to wrong side at notches, and press.

**8**

With right sides together and using a 13mm (½in) seam allowance, sew vest side fronts to vest back at shoulder and side seams. Repeat to assemble vest lining.

**9**

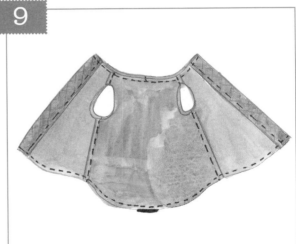

With right sides together and using a 1cm (⅜in) seam allowance, sew vest lining to vest front facings. Fold the front facings backward at notches as shown, and sew vest to lining at neck seam (sandwiching hood in between), and hem (sandwiching the tail in between). Turn right side out through an armhole.

**10**

With right sides together and using a 6mm (¼in) seam allowance, sew little black claw fronts to claw backs. Trim seam allowance to 3mm (⅛in), turn right side out, and stuff with cotton batting. Use a chopstick to push batting into the point of each claw.

**11**

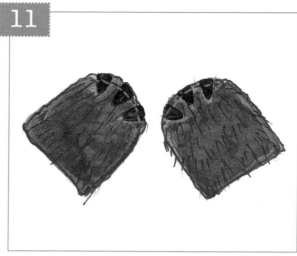

Position claws at notches on fronts of fur paws; baste in place through all thicknesses.

**12**

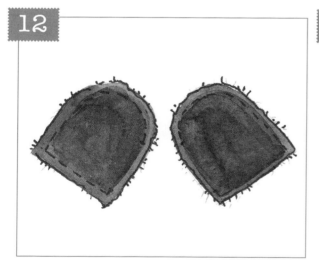

With right sides together, sew pocket linings to paws, leaving a 1cm (⅜in) seam allowance and leaving open between notches. Turn to right side, fold raw edges of openings to inside, and pin closed.

**13**

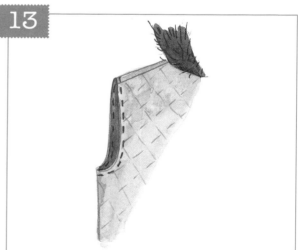

Fold 1cm (⅜in) of each armhole opening to wrong side, both lining and vest. Match underarm and shoulder seams and pin. Carefully stitch lining to vest all the way around each armhole a scant 6mm (¼in) from edge. Topstitch hem 6mm (¼in) from edge.

**14**

Position paws on vest side fronts as indicated on pattern; pin securely in place. Folding the fur pile back at the edges, topstitch paw pockets in place 3mm (⅛in) from the edge, sewing through all layers (paw pockets, vest, and vest lining). Mark and make buttonholes on left side front. Mark button placement on right side front. Sew buttons in place on right side front. Call your little bear out of hibernation and button them into their new vest – time for a walk in the woods!

# Cosy Koala Hat

SIZE:
medium
LEVEL:
intermediate

A happy little hat as warm as it is adorable, this koala helps teach little ones that it can be fun to put on a hat in the cold! Made from wool felt and lined with soft quilted fleece, it's sure to bring a smile.

## You will need

**Grey wool felt** – 45cm (½yd) – Cut 2×A, B, C, 4×D, E, F

**White wool felt** – 22cm (¼yd) – Cut G, 2×H, 2×I

**Black wool felt** – 7.5cm (3in) square scrap – Cut J

**Fleece or sherpa fabric** for lining – 45cm (½yd) – Cut K, 2×L

**Fusible fleece** – 45cm (½yd) – Cut 2×A, B, C

**Half-ball (or similar) buttons** for eyes – 2

**Velcro** – 5cm (2in) piece

**Thread** to match all colours of wool felt

See pattern guide on page 115

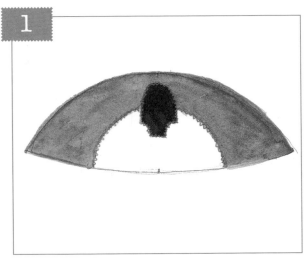

Following package instructions, iron fusible fleece to wrong sides of hood sides and centre, as well as koala muzzle (nose and cheek section). Position white cheek shape on top of muzzle; secure with glue. Using a zigzag or appliqué stitch, sew in place. Position nose, glue it, and zigzag stitch in place with matching thread.

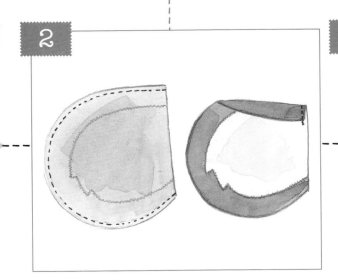

Position white ear centres on right side of ears, glue in place; zigzag stitch edges in place using matching thread. With right sides together, sew ear backs to ear fronts with a 6mm (¼in) seam allowance. Turn right side out and press. Fold top edge of ear down at notch and baste in place.

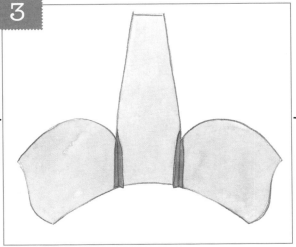

With right sides together, sew koala hat sides to centre from front point to notch using a 6mm (¼in) seam allowance. Press seams open. Matching notches, sew muzzle to hat sides and centre using a 6mm (¼in) seam allowance; press seam open.

**4**

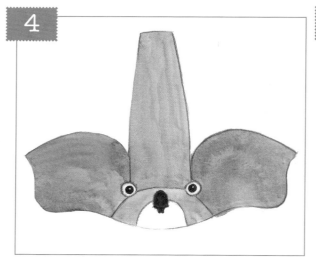

Position white oval eye bases at intersections of side, centre, and muzzle seam; secure in place with glue. Zigzag stitch in place with matching thread. Position button eyes on eye bases and sew in place.

**5**

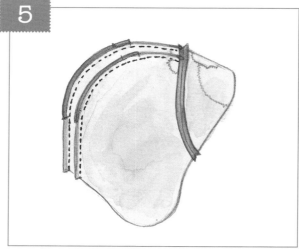

Matching notches, pin and then baste koala ears to hat sides. Then finish sewing hat sides to hat centre. Turn right side out.

**6**

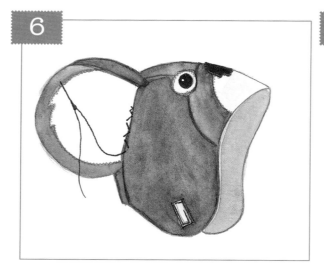

You may invisibly hand stitch the ears to the sides of the head 2.5cm (1in) from where they are attached to the hat, to position them closer to the head. Simply sew through the inside of the hat and catch only the front of each ear in stitching. Trim long edges from hook section of Velcro. Stitch in place on right side of hat.

**7**

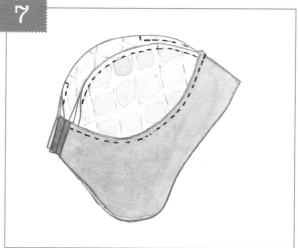

Sew hat lining centre to lining sides (6mm/¼in seam allowance); leave open between notches. Sew facing closed at centre back (6mm/¼in allowance), press seam open. Match notches on facing and lining; sew (6mm/¼in allowance).

**8**

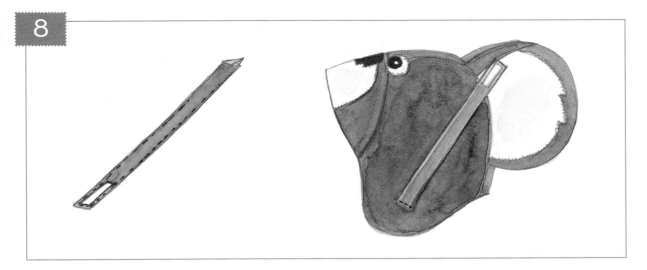

Fold 6mm (¼in) to wrong side of each long side of the chin strap, and press. Topstitch all sides of chin strap 6mm (¼in) from edge. Trim long edges from loop side of Velcro, position on one end of chin strap, and hold in place with dab of fabric glue. Topstitch in place. Position chin strap on left side of hat as shown. Sew in place with a seam 6mm (¼in) from edge, through all thicknesses. Pin to hat to keep out of way during next step.

**9**

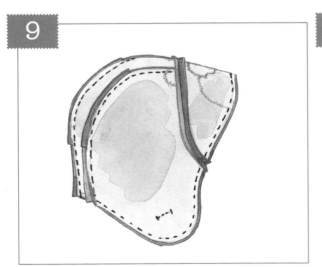

With right sides together, fit hat lining with facing inside hat. Match notches, and sew together using a 6mm (¼in) seam allowance. Turn right side out through opening in left lining seam.

**10**

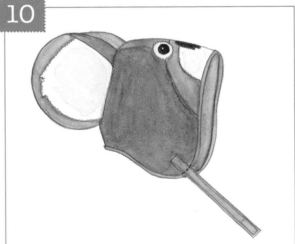

To create a 'faux piping', roll edge of facing a scant 6mm (¼in) to outside edge of hat, and stitch in ditch a scant 6mm (¼in) from edge through all thicknesses. Invisibly hand stitch the opening in the lining closed. Unpin and fold chin strap down; stitch in place in ditch formed where binding meets hat.

SIZE:
medium
LEVEL:
beginner

# Little Leopard Skirt

There is a pretty kitty camouflaged by the leopard print of this skirt! Her face is in the front, and her swishy tail follows wherever she goes. A quick project that can be completed in only a few hours, try other printed fabrics for a variety of cats. How about a floral pinwale corduroy or polka dot velveteen kitty?

## You will need

**Leopard print cotton velveteen** (or similar) – 90cm (1yd) – Cut A, 2×B, 2×C, 2×D, 2×E, F, G, 2×H

**Pink taffeta** – 11cm (⅛yd) or scrap – Cut 2×H, L

**Black velveteen or similar** – 12.5cm (5in) square scrap – Cut 2×I, 2×J, K

**Paper-backed fusible bonding web** (such as Heat N Bond or Stitch Witchery) – 12.5cm (5in) square scrap

**Buttons** for eyes – 2, 1.3cm (½in) in diameter

**2cm- (¾in-) wide elastic** – 45cm (18in) – Cut M

**Thread** to match velveteen, taffeta and black velveteen

**See pattern guide on page 115**

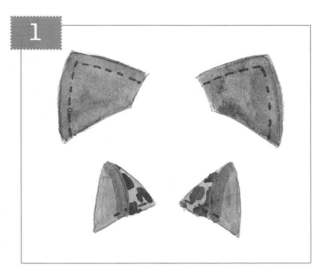

With right sides together, sew pink taffeta ear fronts to velveteen ear backs using a 6mm (¼in) seam allowance. Clip corners, turn, and press. Fold inside corner of each ear as shown and baste in place.

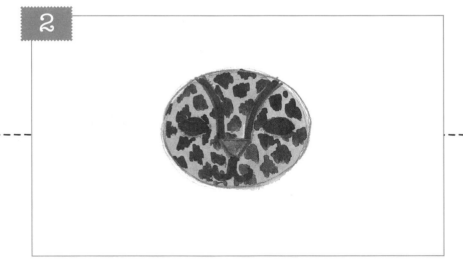

Trace the pattern piece for the leopard face onto the paper-backed fusible adhesive. Fuse it to the back of the leopard face. Apply adhesive to a 10cm by 15cm (4in by 6in) square of black velveteen and a 5cm (2in) square of pink taffeta. Transfer the patterns for the nose stripes, eyes, and mouth onto the paper backing of the black velveteen; cut out. Transfer the pattern for the nose onto the paper backing of the pink taffeta; cut out. Peel away backing from all pieces.

**3**

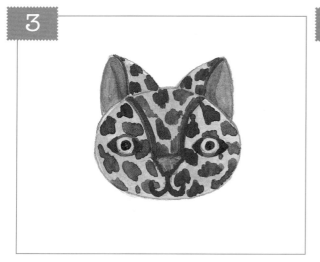

**4**

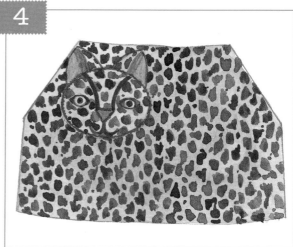

Position nose stripes, eyes, nose, and mouth on the right side of the leopard face and fuse in place with an iron (use a pressing cloth). Peel paper backing from the back of the leopard face. Using a zigzag or appliqué stitch, neatly sew the facial features in place. Position ears behind face and pin to hold in place.

Position face and ears on leopard skirt front as indicated on pattern, and carefully fuse in place. Sew in place by stitching around the circumference of the face using a zigzag or appliqué stitch.

**5**

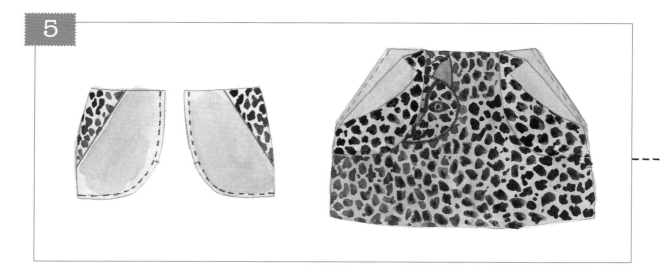

With right sides together, sew pockets to pocket linings, matching notches. Turn pockets so that right sides are facing out and position on skirt front as shown; sew in place. Fold pockets back along these seams to inside of skirt, turning so that pocket right sides are in again. Topstitch pocket front edge 6mm (¼in) from edge. Baste pocket linings in place along waist and side seam.

**6**

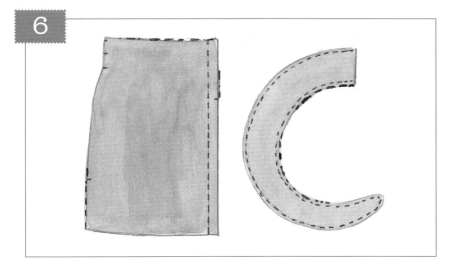

Sew tail front to tail back with right sides together as shown, using a scant 6mm (¼in) seam allowance. Turn to right side and press. Position tail between notches on skirt side back, and place second skirt side back on top, matching notches. Sew centre back seam so that tail is sandwiched between. Press seam open.

**7**

To create casing for elastic: Fold top edge of skirt 6mm (¼in) to inside and press. Fold again at notch 3cm (1¼in) to inside and press. Topstitch in place 3mm (⅛in) from each fold to create casing.

**8**

Use the pattern to cut lightweight fusible interfacing to match the skirt front waistband. Fuse it to the back of the front waistband. Fold top edge of waistband 6mm (¼in) to wrong side and press. Fold again in half at notches and press; unfold. With right sides together, matching notches, sew long unfolded edge of waistband to skirt front waist through all thicknesses.

**9**

Cut elastic to length and use a loop turner to pull through casing on skirt back. Baste ends in place to secure. With right sides together and matching notches, sew skirt front to skirt back through all thicknesses, keeping front waistband free as shown.

**10**

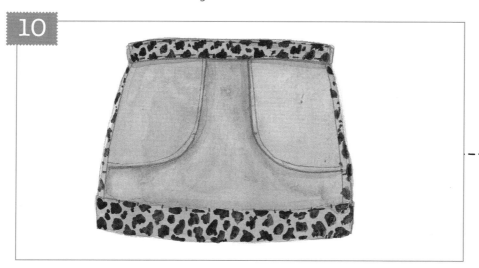

Fold front waistband to inside of skirt, enclosing elastic ends at side seams.

**11**

From the right side, stitch in the ditch of the seam where the waistband was sewn to the skirt front to secure the waistband in place. Topstitch side of waistband in place to hide elastic. Add a decorative topstitch 6mm (¼in) from top edge of waistband and 6mm (¼in) from bottom edge of waistband. Fold hem 6mm (¼in) to inside, and press. Fold again 3cm (1¼in) to inside and sew in place, either by hand or using a machine blind hemstitch.

# Elephant Friends Shirt

SIZE:
large
LEVEL:
beginner

It's hard to get little guys out of their T-shirts in the summer, but with the help of these two friendly elephants your young man will be well dressed in a snap! Make the shirt from a cool cotton print or madras plaid and pair it with khakis for a polished look. Know a little girl who's an elephant lover? Try pink elephants on a polka dot background, and thread elastic through the sleeve hems for puffed sleeves.

## You will need

**Cotton print fabric** – 180cm (2yd) – Cut D, 2×E, 2×F, 2×G, 2×H, 2×I

**Solid cotton fabric** for elephants – 45cm (½yd) – Cut 2×A, 2×B, 4×C

**White linen (or similar) scrap** for tusks, if you would like to include them – Cut to desired size and shape

**Thread** to match all cotton fabrics

**Contrasting colour embroidery floss** for eyes and tail – 1 skein

**Buttons** – 4, 1.3cm (½in) in diameter

**See pattern guide on page 120**

Position elephant appliqués on side fronts and back, as indicated, and pin securely in place. Appliqués do not include tusks, so cut from white linen and include, if desired. Zigzag or appliqué stitch in place, smoothing the fabric as you go so that there are no wrinkles.

With right sides together, stitch ear fronts to ear backs using a 6mm (¼in) seam allowance. Clip curves, turn ears right side out, press. Topstitch ears around edges a scant 3mm (⅛in) from edge. Position ears on elephants with right sides together; topstitch in place through all thicknesses. Fold ears back into final position, press, topstitch in place.

**3**

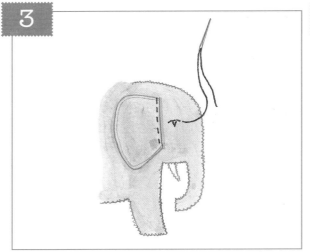

Thread a small embroidery needle with embroidery floss that contrasts with elephants. Hand embroider eyes using a backstitch, as above.

**4**

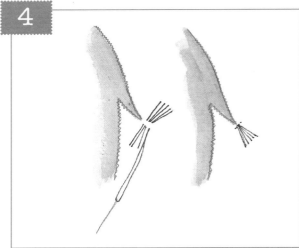

To create tail tassels, use same embroidery floss and tapestry needle to stitch through base of tail, and clip thread leaving 5cm (2in) on either end of stitch. Repeat several times until desired thickness of tail is created. Fold upper floss strands down, and machine stitch backward and forward several times to secure tassel.

**5**

To make pleats on shirt back, fold along yoke edge as indicated, matching notches, and baste in place 13mm (½in) from edge.

**6**

With right sides of each yoke piece facing each other, sandwich shirt back between two shirt yokes and sew in place using a 13mm (½in) seam allowance. Fold yoke pieces up and press. Topstitch along yokes just above seam 3mm (⅛in) from edge.

Lay bottom yoke on top of shirt side fronts and sew shoulder seams as shown using a 13mm (½in) seam allowance. Press shoulder seams toward back. Press 1cm (⅜in) to wrong side of shoulder seams on top yoke, fold top yoke in place on top of bottom yoke, and topstitch shoulder seams through all thicknesses.

With right sides together and matching notches, stitch sleeves into body of shirt. Press seams toward sleeves.

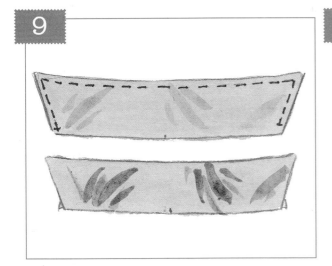

From notch, sew top collar to bottom collar with right sides together, using a 13mm (½in) seam allowance. Turn to right side, press. Fold 1cm (⅜in) of neck side top collar to wrong side and press.

Fold outside edge of front facings 6mm (¼in) to wrong side and press, fold 6mm (¼in) to wrong side again and press; topstitch in place.

**11**

**12**

Matching notches at centre back neck, sew under collar to shirt neck with right sides together, using a 13mm (½in) seam allowance.

Repeat with cuffs. Fold top edge of front facings 1cm (⅜in) to wrong side and press. Fold front facings to wrong side at notches. Stitch along neckline as illustrated using a 13mm (½in) seam allowance, sandwiching under collar between shirt body and facings, but keeping top collar free.

**13**

**14**

Turn facings to inside. Topstitch top collar to bottom collar 3mm (⅛in) from seam through all thicknesses as shown. Topstitch shoulder seams 3mm (⅛in) from seam, securing folded top edge of front facings in seam.

Using a 13mm (½in) seam allowance, with right sides together, sew sleeve and underarm seams, pivoting at underarm.

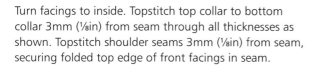

**15**

Hem sleeves by folding 6mm (¼in) to wrong side, then 13mm (½in), and topstitching 1cm (⅜in) from the edge. Hem shirt bottom by folding 6mm (¼in) to wrong side and pressing, then 2.5cm (1in) to wrong side, and stitching 2cm (¾in) from edge. Make buttonholes on left front placket as marked on pattern. Sew buttons on right front placket to correspond with buttonholes. Call your little adventurer and tell them it's time for a safari!

# Woodland Animals

# Bunny Coat

This little topper is great for spring days when it's not warm enough to go without a jacket, but not cold enough for a heavy coat. Charming for an egg hunt, make it in grey or brown wool for little boy rabbits. Sewn from a soft cashmere woven in the smallest size, it makes a memorable gift for a mother-to-be.

## You will need

**Wool woven fabric** – 180cm (2yd) – Cut 2×A, 2×B, C, D, E, F, 2×G, 2×H, 4×I, J

**Cotton print fabric** – 180cm (2yd) – Cut 2×K, L, 2×M, N, 2×O, 2×P, 2×Q, R

**Thread** to match wool fabric

**Large metal snap** – 1

**Fluffy yarn** for tail – 1 skein

**Cardboard** for tail assembly – 9cm by 15cm (3½in by 6in)

**See pattern guide on page 116**

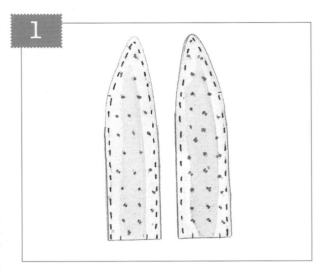

With right sides together, using a 6mm (¼in) seam allowance, sew the bunny ear fronts to the bunny ear backs, leaving them open at the notched end. Turn to right side and press.

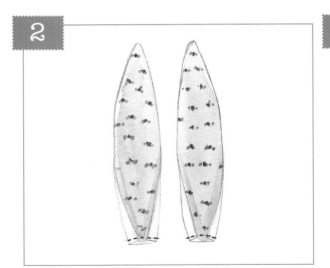

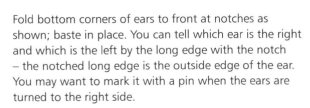

Fold bottom corners of ears to front at notches as shown; baste in place. You can tell which ear is the right and which is the left by the long edge with the notch – the notched long edge is the outside edge of the ear. You may want to mark it with a pin when the ears are turned to the right side.

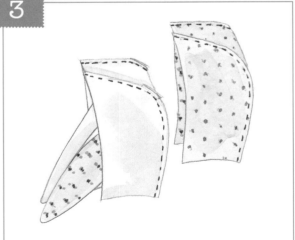

With right sides together, using a 6mm (¼in) seam allowance, sew lining side hoods to lining centre hood. Pin ears in place between notches on hood sides with print facing the right side of hood sides. Sew hood centre to hood sides with right sides together using a 6mm (¼in) seam allowance, sandwiching ears in place.

**4**

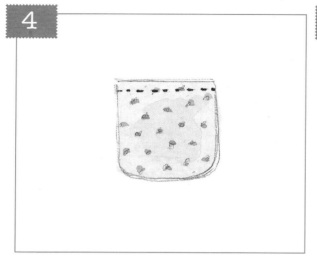

With right sides together, sew pocket front to pocket back along top edge. Turn to right side.

**5**

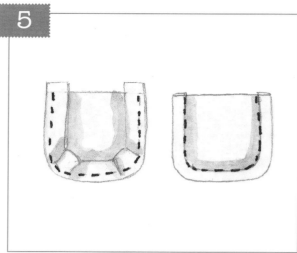

With a 13mm (½in) seam allowance and right sides together, sew bias binding to three unfinished sides of pocket through all thicknesses as shown. Fold bias binding around edges of pocket to lining side, folding ends neatly down at top. Press in place, and stitch in the ditch to secure.

**6**

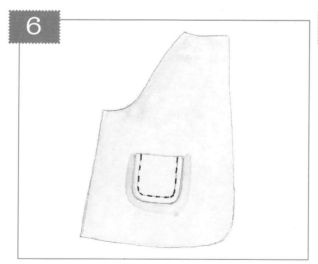

Place pocket as shown on right side front, in position indicated on pattern piece. Sew again in seam ditch through all thicknesses.

**7**

With right sides together and matching notches, sew sleeve fronts to coat side fronts using a 6mm (¼in) seam allowance. Repeat for lining sleeve fronts and lining side fronts.

**8**

With right sides together and matching notches, sew sleeve backs to coat back using a 6mm (¼in) seam allowance. Repeat for lining sleeve backs and lining coat back.

**9**

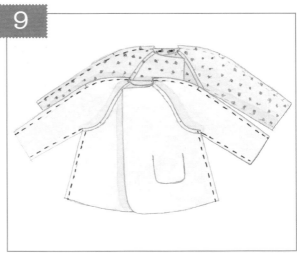

With right sides together and matching notches, sew coat front to coat back at shoulder seams, underarm seams, and side seams using a 13mm (½in) seam allowance. Repeat this step for coat lining shoulder, underarm, and side seams. Turn coat to right side.

**10**

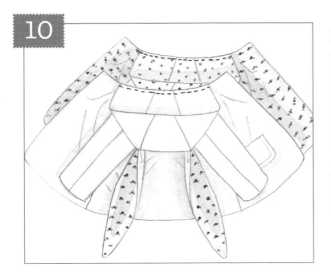

With right sides together and matching notches, sew hood to neck of coat. Repeat for hood lining and coat lining. Carefully fit lining into coat, matching and pinning outside edges.

### Note

If you have a serger, you may wish to serge the inside long edge of bias binding. Alternately you can finish with a zigzag stitch on a regular sewing machine. However, as bias edges do not fray, it is also perfectly acceptable to leave the edge unfinished.

**11**

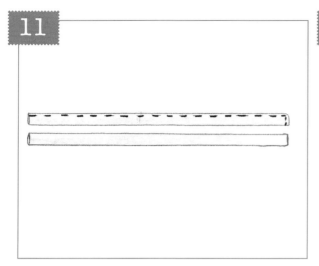

To create ties for closures, fold each tie in half lengthwise with right sides together. Sew long ends and one short edge together. Use a loop turner to turn to right side, press. Pin two in place at notches on right side front of coat, matching raw edge to raw edge of coat.

**12**

Beginning at left side seam, with right sides together, in the same manner as sleeve hems, sew bias binding using a 13mm (½in) seam allowance to bottom edge of coat, around left front, around hood, down right side front edge (sandwiching ties in place), and around front hem and back hem to finish where you began at left side seam.

**13**

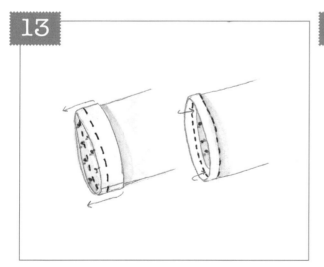

Fold bias to inside and press; stitch in the ditch all the way around to enclose raw edges. Take extra care at curves and corners – the bias will stretch to accommodate them. Fold right side ties toward opening and baste in place.

**14**

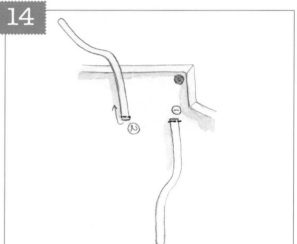

Sew snap in place on left side front and right side front lining in positions indicated on pattern. Sew open ends of remaining ties in place as shown (1), in positions indicated on left side front pattern piece. Fold toward open edge and stitch again to conceal raw edge (2).

**15**

To create bunny tail, wrap fluffy yarn around a piece of cardboard 9cm (3½in) wide and 15cm (6in) long. Wrap many times until yarn is about 2.5cm (1in) thick on either side of cardboard (number of wraps will vary based on thickness of yarn used). Use a tapestry needle to thread a double length of yarn under all layers as shown; tie in a tight, secure knot.

**16**

Cut yarn through all thicknesses at edge opposite knot to release cardboard. Fluff up tail; trim ends if uneven. Hand stitch in place on back of coat, catching centre knot of tail in stitching. Alternatively, stitch to large safety pin and pin in place, allowing for easy removal for cleaning.

# Raccoon Vest

Raccoons are clever rascals indeed, with their masklike facial markings and proclivity to get into anything and everything. This little raccoon is masquerading as a mild-mannered herringbone vest. The removable tail and fleece lining keep it both fun and functional!

## You will need

**Wool tweed fabric** or similar – 90cm (1yd) – Cut A, 2×B, C, D, E, F, G, 2×H, 2×I

**Fleece fabric** for lining – 90cm (1yd) – Cut 2×Q, R, S, 2×T

**Cream wool felt** for face – 22cm (¼yd) – Cut 2×I, 2×J, 2×K, 2×L

**Black wool felt or woven wool fabric** for face and tail – 11cm (⅛yd) – Cut M, 2×N, 2×O, P

**Thread** to match grey, cream, and black

**Face template** – V – Do not cut; use for reference when placing features

**Fusible fleece interfacing** or similar – 22cm (¼yd) – Cut U

**Buttons** – 2, 2.5cm (1in) in diameter for eyes, 4, 1.5cm (⅝in) in diameter for front

**Ribbon or cord** for drawstring – 135cm (1½yd)

**Yarn** for tail – ½ skein black, ½ skein cream

**Velcro** – One 7.5cm by 1.5cm (3in by ⅝in) piece

**Tracing paper** for tail assembly

**Cardboard** for tail assembly

**See pattern guide on page 118**

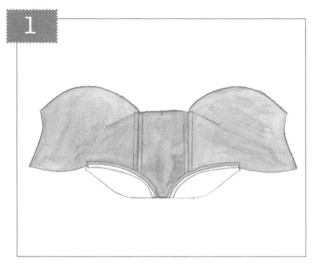

With right sides together and using a 6mm (¼in) seam allowance, sew hood sides to hood centre front, stopping at darts. Press seams open. With right sides together and using a 6mm (¼in) seam allowance, sew raccoon cheeks to hood as shown. Press seams open.

Position black 'eye masks' on top of cream eye accents as indicated on pattern, secure with a dab of fabric glue, and zigzag or appliqué stitch in place. Position cream eye shapes and black nose, secure with glue, and appliqué in place. Cut fusible fleece or other fusible stabiliser to match raccoon hood interfacing piece. Position on wrong side of raccoon hood face 13mm (½in) from front edge and fuse in place with iron. Position button eyes on face; hand stitch in place.

**3**

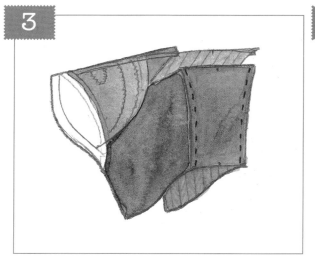

Sew hood sides to hood centre back with right sides together and using a 6mm (¼in) seam allowance.

**4**

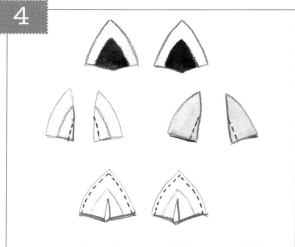

Using a zigzag or appliqué stitch, sew black ear centres onto right side of ear fronts. Fold each ear front in half with right sides together, and stitch darts through all layers. Repeat for ear backs. With right sides together, using a 6mm (¼in) seam allowance, sew ear fronts to ear backs. Turn and press.

**5**

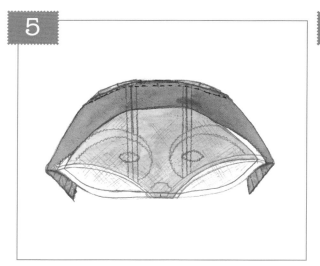

Position ears on top of raccoon head between notches as shown (fronts of ears should face raccoon face) and pin in place. Sew seam along hood top closed, sandwiching raccoon ears in between.

**6**

Sew hood lining side fronts to centre, right sides together, using 6mm (¼in) seam allowance. Right sides together, using 6mm (¼in) seam allowance, sew hood facing to lining. Right sides together, sew hood to lining around face opening using 6mm (¼in) seam allowance. Turn to right side, fit lining into hood; press seam flat.

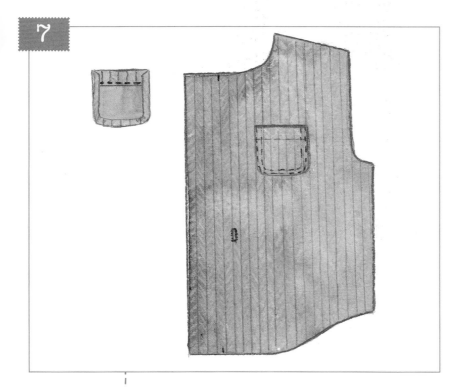

**7**

To create openings for the drawstring to pass through, make one buttonhole on each side front in position indicated on pattern. Fold top edge of pocket 18mm (¾in) to wrong side, stitch in place 13mm (½in) from edge. Carefully press remaining three edges of pocket 6mm (¼in) to wrong side. Position on left side front as indicated in pattern, stitch in place a scant 3mm (⅛in) from edge. Stitch again 6mm (¼in) from first line of stitching.

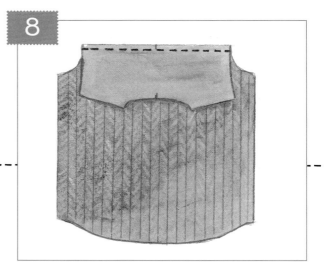

**8**

With right sides together, sew back yoke to lower back using a 13mm (½in) seam allowance. Press seam open.

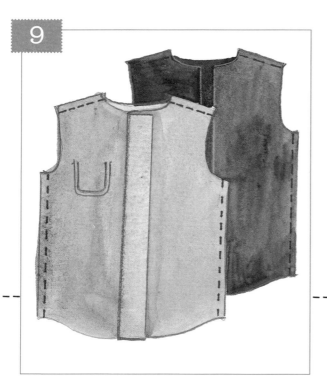

Fold facings on side fronts to wrong side at notches; press. With right sides together, sew vest back to vest side fronts at shoulder and side seams, using a 13mm (½in) seam allowance. Press seams open. Repeat for vest lining back and side fronts. From right side, topstitch shoulder and side seams of vest 13mm (½in) from seam.

With right sides together and matching notches at centre back neck, pin hood to vest body. Stitch through all thicknesses, using a 6mm (¼in) seam allowance.

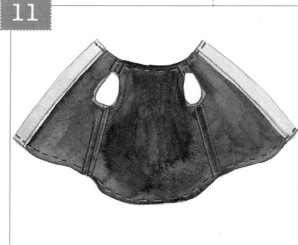

Sew lining to front facings, right sides together (13mm/½in seam allowance). Fold at facings and sew neck seam (6mm/¼in seam allowance), sandwiching hood between lining and vest. Sew vest to lining at hem (6mm/¼in seam allowance). Turn right side out through armhole; press seams flat. Topstitch hem 13mm (½in) from edge.

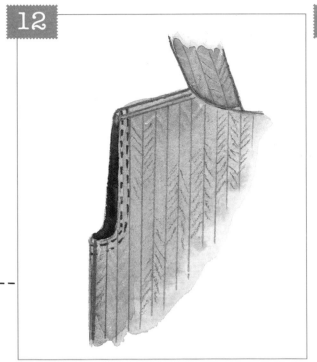

Fold 1cm (⅜in) of armholes of vest to wrong side and press; fold 13mm (½in) of lining armholes to wrong side. Matching vest armhole to lining armhole to create a finished edge, sew vest to lining a scant 3mm (⅛in) from edge. Topstitch 6mm (¼in) away from first seam.

To create casing for drawstring, stitch two parallel seams in positions indicated on pattern, one above and one below buttonholes. Use a loop turner or safety pin to pull cording or ribbon through casing, in one buttonhole and out the other. Make buttonholes on left side front in positions indicated on pattern; hand sew corresponding buttons on right side. To make a place to attach the raccoon tail, machine stitch the loop side of a 7.5cm (3in) piece of 1.5cm- (⅝in-) wide Velcro inside vest back in position indicated on pattern.

## Note

Take your time while finishing the armholes for the best results. Fold both edges to the inside and pin together at the side seam and the top of the shoulder seam, then work your way around the rest of the armhole, pinning in place. Machine stitch slowly and remove the pins as you go, maintaining an even 3mm (⅛in) distance from the edge.

**14**

To assemble the tail, fold the tail 'stem' lengthwise with right sides together and stitch a scant 6mm (¼in) from edge and across one end. Stitch up the open side to create a double thick felt strip. Place 7.5cm (¼in) piece of 1.5cm- (⅝in-) wide Velcro at top of stem and topstitch in place around edges.

**15**

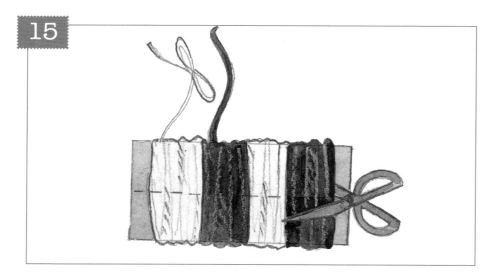

Cut a piece of cardboard 15cm (6in) wide and 30cm (12in) long. Wrap black yarn around cardboard roughly 30 times, then wrap cream-coloured yarn around the bottom of the cardboard roughly 30 times. Repeat 30 times with black, then 30 times with cream to make stripes. Yarn should feel about 1.5cm (⅝in) thick on each side. Cut wrapped yarn down the middle of the front of the board, releasing it. Cut down centre of yarn again as it lies flat, so you are left with two rows of 15cm- (6in-) long pieces.

**16**

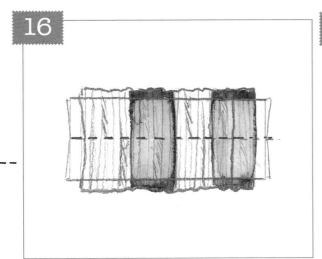

**17**

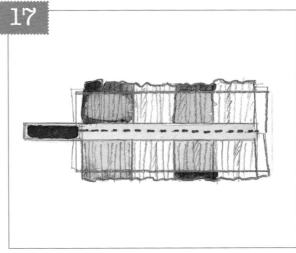

Cut four pieces tracing paper 30cm (12in) long and 10cm (4in) wide. Lay a piece on work table and position yarn pieces in one column, with about 2.5cm (1in) space top and bottom. Layer paper on top; secure all layers with quilting pins. Sew straight down the centre. Do not remove paper. Repeat for second batch.

Lay tail stem along stitching line of one section of tail yarn; stitch through all layers down the middle, leaving 2.5cm (1in) space at top open end. Lay second section of yarn on top of tail stem, so it is sandwiched between the two layers of yarn. Stitch on top of centre seam, through all layers. Go slowly, as this will be quite thick.

**18**

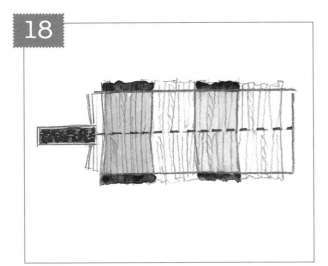

Gently tear away all tracing paper and shake tail to fluff. Trim yarn ends to create a pleasing raccoon tail shape. Velcro in place on vest, and get ready for some raccoon mischief!

# Cute Hoot Owl Hat

Super cute, this hat is a hoot! Crafted of soft wool felt, this winter warmer features an appliquéd face, button eyes, and 'feather' tassels. Keeping little ears toasty, it stays in place with an adjustable chin strap owlets can close themselves. Wonderful for cold weather or dress-up play indoors!

## You will need

**Pink wool felt** for outer hood – 45cm (½yd) – Cut 2×A, B

**Peach wool felt** for strap, binding, tassels and eye bases – 11cm (⅛yd) – Cut E, F, 2×G, 10×H

**Yellow wool felt** for beak and eyelashes – 12.5cm (5in) square scrap – Cut I, 2×J

**Green wool felt** for outer eye base – 25cm by 12.5cm (10in by 5in) scrap – Cut 2×L

**Blue wool felt** for eye middle – 20cm by 10cm (8in by 4in) scrap – Cut 2×K

**Cotton print** for lining – 45cm (½yd) – Cut 2×C, D

**Fusible fleece interfacing** – 45cm (½yd) – Cut 2×A, B

**Face template** – Do not cut; use for reference when placing features

**Buttons** for eyes – 2, 2.5cm (1in) in diameter

**Velcro** – 5cm (2in) piece

**Thread** to match all colours of wool felt

**Fabric glue**

**See pattern guide on page 121**

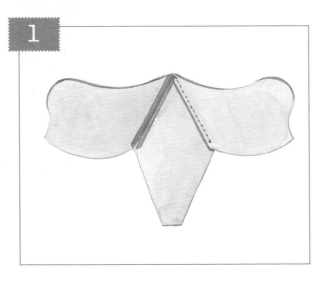

**1**

Following package instructions, iron fusible fleece to wrong sides of hat sides and centre. With right sides together, sew owl hat sides to centre from front point to notch using a 6mm (¼in) seam allowance. Press seams open.

**2**

Layer strips for tassels to create two small fans. Baste each tassel together at the base. Position blue eye centres on top of peach eye circles and tuck yellow eyelashes between; glue. Using zigzag or appliqué stitch, sew eye centres in place, going over the yellow eyelashes. Using more dabs of fabric glue, position peach eye circles on top of green eye shapes and stitch in place (take care not to catch the eyelashes in stitching) using thread to match the peach eye circles.

**3**

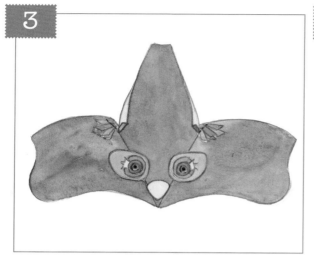

Position beak on outside of owl hat, glue. Zigzag in place using thread to match. Position assembled eyes on hat, glue, and stitch with matching thread. Press eyes from the wrong side of the fabric. Place button eyes in centre of blue circles, and hand stitch. Place ear tassels on corners of hat between notches, and baste in place.

**4**

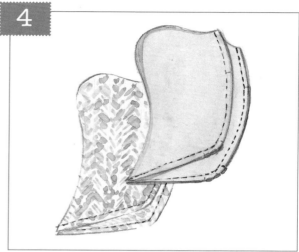

With right sides together and matching notches, sew remaining portion of front seam closed through tassels (6mm/¼in seam allowance), then sew down back seams of hat, sewing through tassels to secure them in place. Press seams open; turn hat to right side. Sew lining and press seams open.

**5**

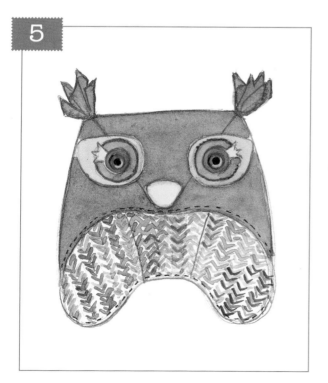

Sew hat lining sides to hat lining centre (6mm/¼in seam allowance), matching notches and pressing seams open. With wrong sides together, fit lining into the hat, matching seams. Trim any excess lining from edges, and baste lining into place around all raw edges a scant 6mm (¼in) from edge.

**6**

Fold 13mm (½in) of one end of felt binding to wrong side, with edge at centre back of right side of hat, and pin in place. Pin remaining binding in place all the way around hat and overlap ends, centre back. Sew in place with a 1cm (⅜in) seam allowance. Fold bias trim to inside, and press. From right side, stitch in the ditch where the binding meets the hat all the way around through all layers. Fold 6mm (¼in) to wrong side of each long side of the chin strap, and press. Topstitch all sides of chinstrap 6mm (¼in) from edge. Trim long edges from loop side of Velcro, position on one end of chin strap, and hold in place with dab of fabric glue. Topstitch in place.

**7**

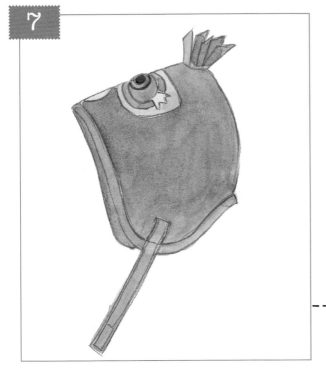

Position chin strap on left side of hat as shown. Sew in place with a seam 6mm (¼in) from edge, through all thicknesses. Fold chin strap down; stitch in place in ditch formed where binding meets hat through all thicknesses. Trim long edges from loop side of Velcro, position on right side of hat as indicated on pattern. Topstitch in place.

# Foxy Scarf

SIZE:
medium
LEVEL:
intermediate

This scarf is a tongue-in-cheek nod to the fox-fur wraps worn by 1930s ladies, but it's a lot friendlier to the foxes! Hidden underneath the cute fox head and fluffy tail are pockets to warm your little one's 'paws'. It is made from cotton velveteen, but fleece or wool can be used for colder weather.

## NOTE

If you are using velvet or velveteen for this project, make sure to use a pressing cloth or press from behind whenever ironing. A terry washcloth works well.

## You will need

**Sienna cotton velveteen** – 1.5m (1⅔yd) – Cut A, B, 4×C, D, 2×E

**Cream cotton velveteen** – 1.5m (1⅔yd) – Cut F, 2×G, 2×H

**Black cotton velveteen** – 25cm (10in) square scrap – Cut I, 2×J, 2×K

**Lining** for inside pockets – Cut 2×G

**Thread** to match all colours of velveteen

**Paper-backed fusible bonding web** (follow manufacturer's instructions for use) – square scrap – Cut I, 2×J

**Brown yarn** – ½ skein

**Cream yarn** – ¼ skein

**Tracing paper** for tail assembly – 4 long pieces

**Cardboard** for making tail – 15cm by 30cm (6in by 12in) piece

**See pattern guide on page 122**

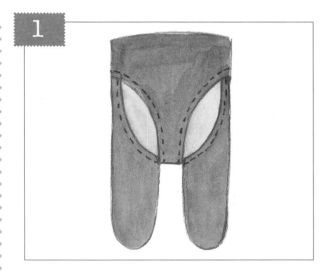

With right sides together and using a 6mm (¼in) seam allowance, sew fox cheeks to fox centre face. Press seams toward cheeks. In the same manner, sew front paws onto front cheeks. Press seams toward cheeks.

Following manufacturer's instructions, iron paper-backed fusible adhesive onto a scrap of black velvet. Transfer eyes and nose onto paper backing, cut, and peel paper off. Position eyes and nose as shown on fox face, and fuse into place with the iron (see note). Using a zigzag or appliqué stitch, sew eyes and nose in place.

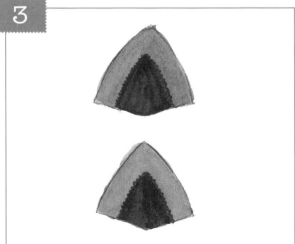

Using a zigzag or appliqué stitch, sew black ear centres onto right side of ear fronts. Sew rows of stitching on front and back paws.

**4**

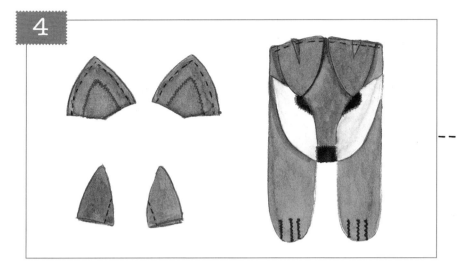

With right sides together, using a 6mm (¼in) seam allowance, sew ear fronts to ear backs. Turn and press. Fold each ear in half with the backs out, and stitch darts through all layers. Position ears on top of fox head as shown and baste in place.

**5**

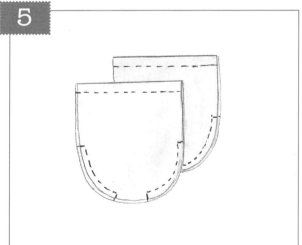

With right sides together, using a 13mm (½in) seam allowance, sew the tops of the hand pockets to pocket lining. Using a 6mm (¼in) seam allowance, sew curved bottoms of hand pockets together between notches. Clip end of stitching to seam. Turn to right side; press.

**6**

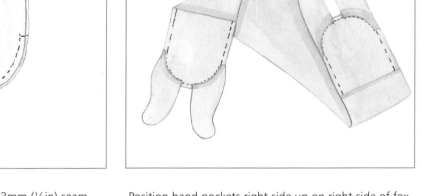

Position hand pockets right side up on right side of fox belly (scarf lining). Baste side edges and space between paws in place using a 1cm (⅜in) seam allowance. Topstitch finished curved edges in place a scant 3mm (⅛in) from edge.

**7**

Cut a piece of sturdy cardboard that is 15cm (6in) wide and roughly 30cm (12in) long. Wrap brown yarn around cardboard roughly 100 times (thicker yarn may require fewer wraps, finer yarn will require more), then wrap cream-coloured yarn around the bottom of the cardboard roughly 30 times. Yarn should feel about 15mm (⅝in) thick on each side of board.

**8**

When yarn is wrapped, use sharp scissors to cut yarn down the middle of the front of the board, releasing yarn. Be careful not to disturb the cut yarn pieces. Use scissors to cut down centre of yarn again as it lies flat, so that you are left with two rows of 15cm- (6in-) long yarn pieces.

**9**

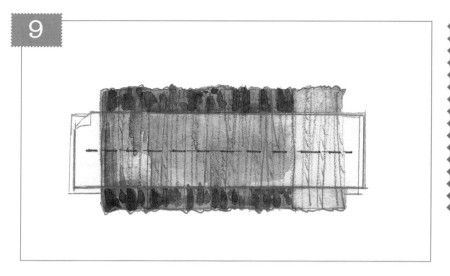

Cut four pieces of tracing paper 30cm (12in) long and about 10cm (4in) wide. Lay one piece on work table and position yarn pieces in one column as shown, with about 2.5cm (1in) of space at top and bottom. Layer second piece of tracing paper on top, and secure all layers in place with quilting pins every few inches. Sew through all layers straight down the centre. Do not remove tracing paper. Repeat for second batch of yarn pieces.

**10**

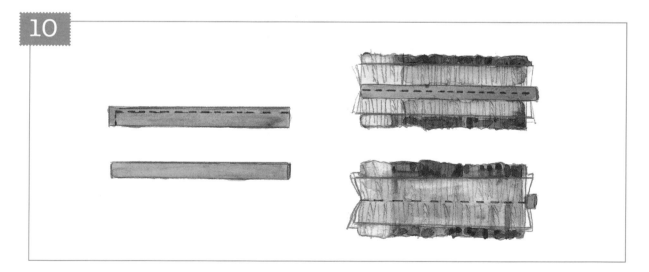

To assemble the tail, fold the tail 'stem' lengthwise with right sides together and stitch a scant 6mm (¼in) from edge and across one end. Turn using a loop turner; press. Lay along stitching line of one section of tail yarn, and stitch through all layers, leaving 2.5cm (¼in) space at top open end. Lay second section of yarn on top, to sandwich tail. Slowly stitch on top of centre seam, through all layers. Tear away paper and shake to fluff. Trim yarn ends.

**11**

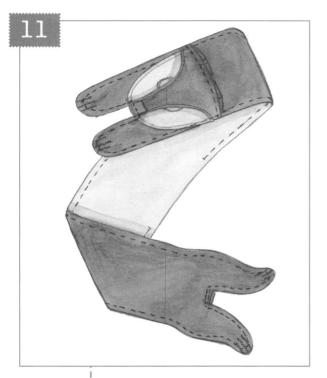

With right sides together, using a 6mm (¼in) seam allowance, sew fox head to fox body. The ears will be sandwiched between the face and body. Position fox tail between fox back legs and baste in place. With right sides together, lay fox body on fox belly, keeping tail out of the way. Match all edges, and pin together. Stitch together using a 1cm (⅜in) seam allowance, leaving opening between notches on side. Clip corners between front and back legs, and clip curves on front paws and back legs. Turn scarf to right side and press. Hand stitch opening in side closed. Introduce your little one to their new foxy friend!

# Butterfly Beach Cape

SIZE:
medium

LEVEL:
intermediate

It's nice to have something cosy to put on after a swim, and this cover-up is sure to delight! Made of absorbent terry cloth, it is as practical as it is pretty. Many fabric stores carry an assortment of colours of terry cloth, but most pattern pieces are small enough to be cut from a bath or beach towel.

## You will need

**Lilac terry cloth** for butterfly wings – 180cm (2yd) – Cut D, 2×E

**Pink terry cloth** for hood, lining, and wing appliqué shapes – 180cm (2yd) – Cut 2×A, 4×B, C, D, 2×E, 4×F, 4×G

**Aqua blue terry cloth** – 45cm (½yd) – Cut 4×H, 4×I

**Green terry cloth** – 22cm (¼yd) – Cut 4×L, 4×J, 4×K

**Yellow terry cloth** – 22cm (¼yd) – Cut 4×O, 4×M, 4×N

**Thread** to match each colour of terry cloth

**Buttons** – 5, 2.5cm (1in) in diameter

**Paper-backed fusible bonding web** for backing wing appliqué pieces (follow manufacturer's instructions for use) – about 90cm (1yd) – Cut 4×F, 4×G, 4×H, 4×I, 4×J, 4×K, 4×L, 4×M, 4×N, 4×O

Wing Appliqué shapes are divided into three groups:

Group 1: M, N

Group 2: G, H, J, L

Group 3: F, I, K, O

**See pattern guide on page 124**

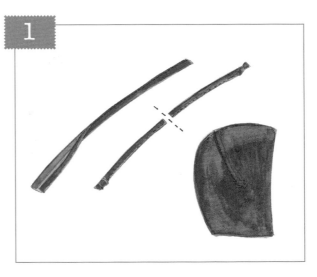

**1**

Fold and press 13mm (½in) to the wrong side of both long sides of the antennae. Stitch closed 3mm (⅛in) from the folded edges. Tie a knot at each end, and cut in half to create two separate antennae. Position each antenna on the right side of each hood side at the notch, and baste in place.

**2**

With right sides together, sew the hood sides to hood centre. Press seams open. Repeat for hood lining sides and hood lining centre. With right sides together, sew hood to hood lining. Turn to right side, and press front seam flat. Topstitch 13mm (½in) from front edge. Baste hood to hood lining at neck edge.

**3**

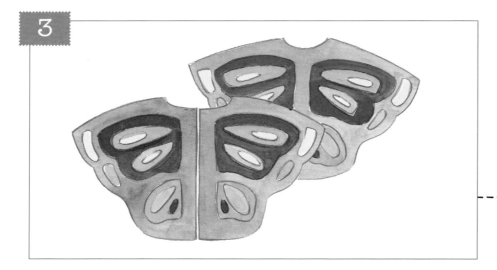

Peel backing from Group 1 wing appliqué shapes. Carefully place them in position on top of Group 2 appliqué shapes, and fuse in place with iron. Position Group 2 shapes on top of Group 3 shapes, and fuse in place with iron. Position Group 3 shapes on the right sides of cape side fronts and cape back, and fuse in place. Using zigzag or appliqué stitch, changing thread to match wing shapes, appliqué each wing shape in place on cape side fronts and cape back. Press from wrong side when complete.

**4**

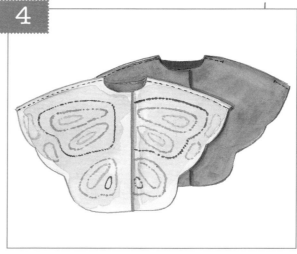

With right sides together, sew cape side fronts to cape back at shoulder seams with a 13mm (½in) seam allowance. Press seams open. With right sides together, sew cape lining side fronts to cape lining back at shoulder seams with a 13mm (½in) seam allowance, leaving an opening between notches. Press seams open.

**5**

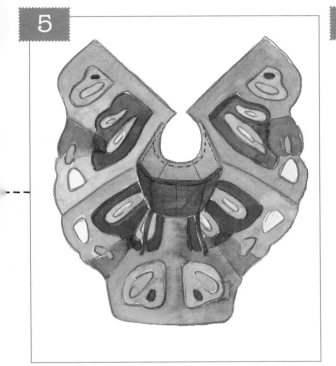

**6**

With right sides together, match the notches of hood centre back neck to cape centre back neck; pin. Pin hood in place on cape at neck. Sew hood to cape with a 6mm (¼in) seam allowance. Sew again to reinforce neck seam. With right sides together, place cape lining on top of cape and pin, matching shoulder seams and all notches. Beginning at centre back neck, sew cape lining to cape all the way around the outside edges with a 6mm (¼in) seam allowance. Clip corners of front opening edges; clip curves. Turn to right side through opening in lining left shoulder. Press lining to inside at all outer edges. Using a whipstitch and matching thread, hand sew opening of lining left shoulder closed.

Starting at right front neck edge, topstitch all the way around the cape 6mm (¼in) from edge. For best results, use your fingers to gently roll the lining to the inside as you topstitch. Make three horizontal buttonholes 18mm (¾in) from edge on right side front, using spacing indicated on pattern. Make two diagonal buttonholes on cape outer side fronts as indicated on pattern. Carefully cut all buttonholes open. Sew corresponding buttons in place on left side front edge, using placement indicated on pattern. Sew buttons to cape back lining at outer sides to correspond with diagonal buttonholes, using placement indicated on pattern. Finally, button your little butterfly into her colourful new cape and watch her fly!

# Farm
# Animals

# Spring Chicken Bonnet

Styled in the manner of a ruffled Victorian baby bonnet, this cheerful chicken is sure to elicit smiles. The frayed edges of the scalloped linen ruffles mimic fluffy feathers. Try making it in felt or fleece for a winter-weather version!

# You will need

**White linen** – 135cm (1½yd) – Cut 9×A, B, 2×C, D, E

**Yellow cotton print** for lining, beak, and feet – 69cm (¾yd) – Cut B, 2×C, 4×F, 2×G

**Thread** to match linen and cotton print

**Lightweight fusible interfacing** to add structure to both outer bonnet and bonnet lining – 69cm (¾yd) – Cut 2×B, 4×C

**Fusible fleece interfacing** or similar – 12.5cm (5in) square scrap

**Buttons** for eyes – 2, 1.3cm (½in) in diameter

**Embroidery floss** or thread for eyelashes – 1 skein

See pattern guide on page 125

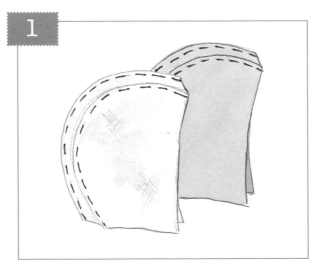

Mark stitching lines for ruffles on right side of bonnet sides and centre, following the spacing indicated on the pattern. Cut bonnet sides and centre from lightweight fusible interfacing, and fuse to wrong side of bonnet sides and centre, following manufacturer's instructions. With right sides together, using a 6mm (¼in) seam allowance, sew sides to centre. Repeat for bonnet lining.

To prepare ruffles, topstitch scalloped edges 6mm (¼in) from edge using a contrasting thread. Make a gathering stitch 3mm (⅛in) from straight edge of each ruffle, leaving threads long, then again 6mm (¼in) from straight edge. Gently pull bobbin threads to gather ruffles.

**3**

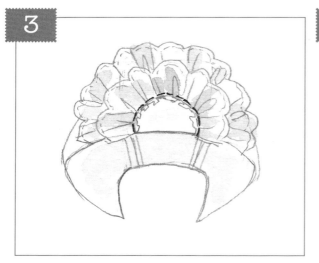

Position gathered edge of ruffle on marked line at the centre front of the bonnet; stitch or zigzag stitch in place. Proceed slowly and carefully. At the end of the bonnet, cut ruffle and begin again at next marked line. When a ruffle ends, overlap the beginning of a new one on top and continue until the end of the row. Repeat.

**4**

Fuse 12.5cm (5in) square of fusible fleece to wrong side of 12.5cm (5in) square of white linen. Cut chicken face out. Fuse scrap of fusible fleece to wrong side of yellow cotton; cut out chicken beak. Cut matching beak out of a non-fused piece of yellow cotton, and cut four (two pairs) chicken feet out of non-fused yellow cotton.

**5**

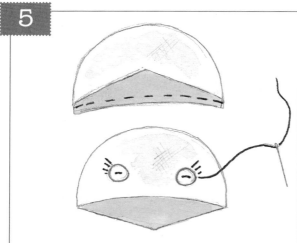

With right sides together, sew beaks together as shown, and sew feet together as shown in step 4. Clip corners and turn to right side; press. With right sides together, sew beak to chicken face. Press seam toward chicken face. Sew buttons in place for chicken eyes, and embroider straight stitches for eyelashes.

**6**

Match notches on open edge of each foot together to make tiny pleats. Pin in place. With right sides together, position feet at notches as shown at bottom edge of hat sides near front, and baste in place.

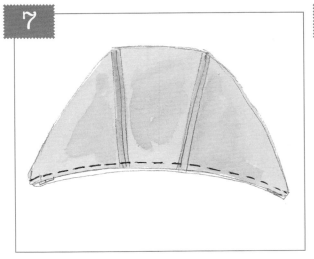

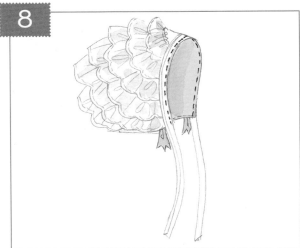

With right sides together, pin bottom edge of bonnet lining to bonnet outer, matching seams. Sew together using a 6mm (¼in) seam allowance, sandwiching feet between the two layers. Turn to right side and fit lining into bonnet. Topstitch bottom neck 3mm (⅛in) from edge through all layers.

Baste lining and hat (including edges of ruffles) together around open face edge. Press 6mm (¼in) to wrong side of long bias for front binding and ties. Find the middle of the binding strip and match with centre front edge of bonnet, right sides and raw edges together. Stitch bias strip around hood opening 6mm (¼in) from edge.

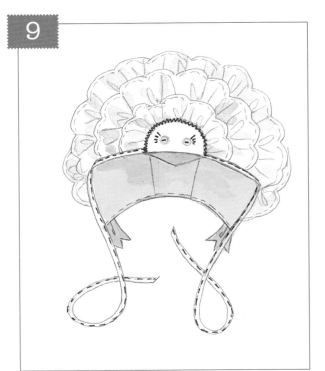

Fold binding to inside and press, then topstitch in place on edge of binding through all thicknesses, securing the folded edge with the seam on the bonnet inside. To create ties fold raw edge 6mm (¼in) to inside and press, then match to previously folded edge and topstitch together. Make a knot at the end of each tie. Position chicken face in place on hat and secure with fabric glue. Topstitch in place around raw edge using zigzag stitch or appliqué. Stitch in ditch across seam connecting beak to face through all layers to further secure it. The ruffles are supposed to have a rustic look, like feathers, so to finish pull threads from raw edges to gently ravel them.

# Little Miss Moo Dress

SIZE: medium
LEVEL: experienced

This crisp, cool sundress is perfect for a picnic in a sunny meadow or a trip to Grandma's farm. Sewn entirely from linen, sweet details like the dimensional flowers in the cow's mouth and the fringed tail that flutters behind are sure to gather smiles!

## You will need

**White linen** – 180cm (2yd) – Cut A, 2×B, 2×C, D, E, 2×F, 2×G, 2×H, I, 2×J

**Black linen** – 45cm (½yd) – Cut 4×K, 2×L, 2×M, 2×N, 2×O, 2×P, Q

**Pink linen** – 11cm (⅛yd) – Cut 2×M, R, 2×S

**Green linen or cotton** – 11cm (⅛yd) – Cut 2×T

**Blue linen or cotton** – 12.5cm (5in) square scrap – Cut 2×U

**Face template** – Do not cut; use for reference when placing features

**Paper-backed fusible bonding web** (such as Heat N Bond or Stitch Witchery) – 25cm (10in) square scrap

**Thread** to match white, black, and pink linen

**Buttons** – 9, 1.3cm (½in) in diameter

**See pattern guide on page 123**

**1**

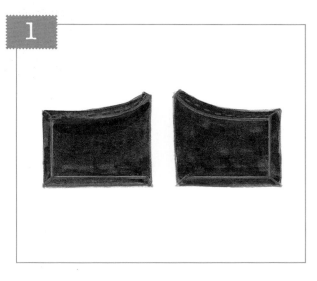

Fold 13mm (½in) to wrong side of top edge of pockets; topstitch in place with a 6mm (¼in) seam allowance. Fold remaining two unnotched edges 13mm (½in) to wrong side.

**2**

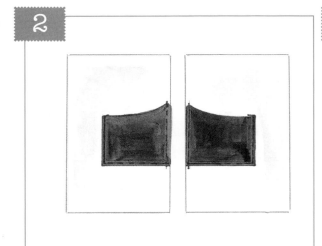

Position on right side of side front skirt sections as shown, matching notches. Topstitch unnotched outer and bottom edges in place; baste inner notched edges to skirt sides.

**3**

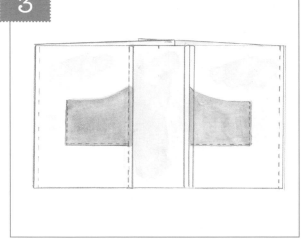

With right sides together, sew skirt sides to skirt centre front.

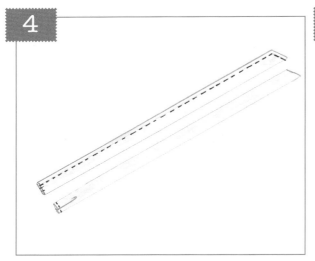

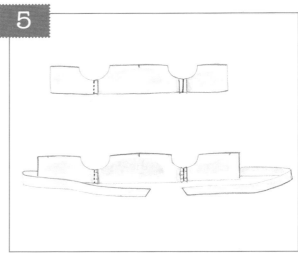

With right sides together, fold each sash section in half lengthwise and sew long edge and slanted end with a 13mm (½in) seam allowance. Using a loop turner, turn each sash right side out and press. Match notches on open end to make a small pleat, and baste in place.

Pin to either side of bodice front. Layer bodice backs on top (right sides together), sandwiching sashes in place. Sew with a 13mm (½in) seam allowance. Press seams open. With right sides together, pin bodice lining backs to bodice lining front and sew in place with a 13mm (½in) seam allowance. Press seams open.

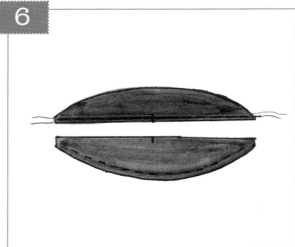

To create shoulder ruffles: With right sides together, sew two shoulder ruffle pieces together along unnotched edge with a 6mm (¼in) seam allowance. Turn to right side; press. Repeat for second shoulder ruffle.

**7**

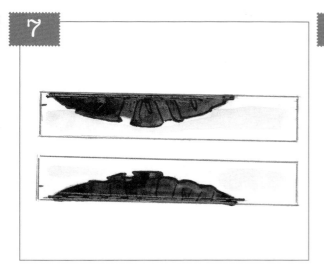

Sew two rows of gathering stitches on notched edges. Pull threads gently to gather. Position gathered edges on shoulder straps, matching notches. Baste in place with a 1cm (⅜in) seam allowance and remove gathering stitches.

**8**

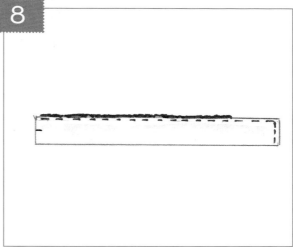

Carefully roll shoulder ruffles into stitched edges to keep out of way. Fold long edges of straps in half, sandwiching ruffles in between. Stitch long edges and unnotched short edge with a 13mm (½in) seam allowance.

**9**

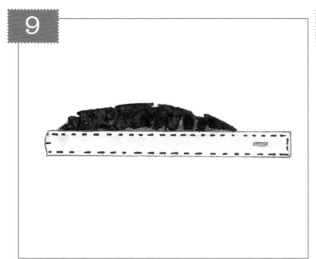

Trim corners, and use a loop turner to turn straps to right side. Press, and topstitch 6mm (¼in) from edge as shown. Sew buttonhole on each strap in position indicated on pattern. You may wish to sew several buttonholes so that the straps may be let out as the child grows.

**10**

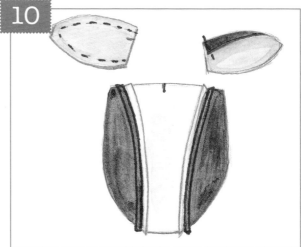

With right sides together, sew pink ear fronts to black ear backs as shown, with a 6mm (¼in) seam allowance. Trim corners; turn each to right side, and press. Fold top edges of ears down at notches and baste in place. With right sides together, sew side front faces to face centre with a 6mm (¼in) seam allowance. Press seams open.

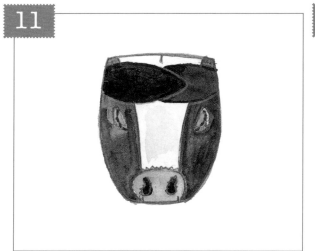

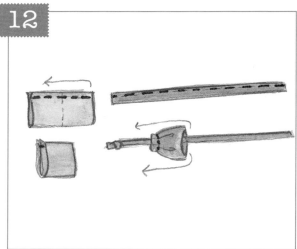

Position ears on right side of cow face; baste in place. Fold eyes in half and gently fray edges. Topstitch in place. Peel backing from wrong side of nose. Iron in place. Zigzag in place on all sides except between notches. Peel backing from double-sided interfacing on nostrils and iron in place. Zigzag stitch around edges.

Fold the flower stems in half lengthwise and sew long edges (6mm/¼ seam). Turn right side out; do not press. Knot one end. Right sides together, sew long edges of pink flowers. Press seams open. Roll/fold flowers in half, wrong sides together. Slide flowers onto stems, pleat raw edge around stem, stitch in place. Flip flowers down.

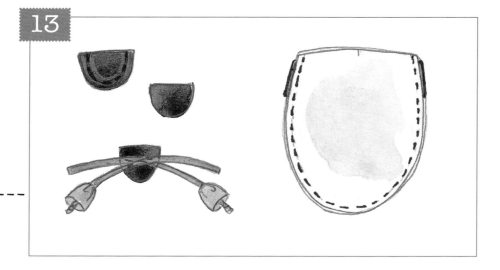

Sew cow chin sections together along curved edge with a 6mm (¼in) seam allowance. Turn to right side; press. Cross flowers over chin section and topstitch in place. Place cow face back on top of cow face and stitch around curved edge as shown, using a 6mm (¼in) seam allowance. Turn to right side and gently press edges, using fingers to roll seams to outer edges to make a nice curved shape.

**14**

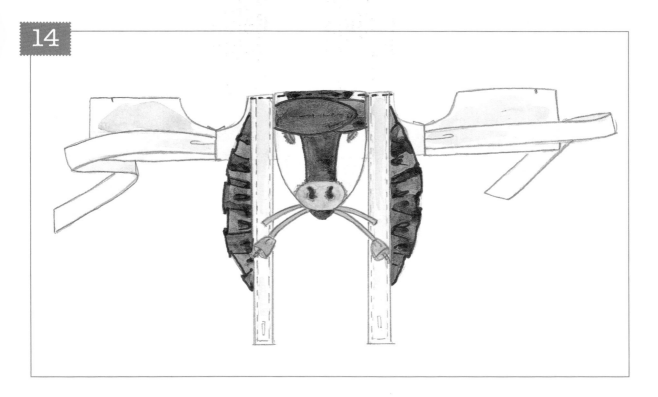

Position chin under face, adjusting spacing for the most pleasing expression. Topstitch in place invisibly, hiding the stitching by going over the appliqué seams of the nostrils. Alternately, catchstitch by hand to sew in place invisibly from the back. Matching centre notch, position face on right side of bodice front, and shoulder straps on each side. Baste with a 1cm (⅜in) seam allowance. Right sides together, stack bodice lining on bodice front, sandwiching face and straps between. Using a 13mm (½in) seam allowance, sew top edge, beginning at notch, around armhole, across front, around other armhole, to notch. Clip corners and curves. Turn to right side; press. Baste bodice front to bodice along skirt edge.

**15**

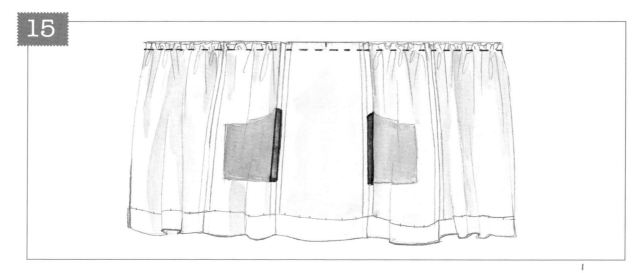

To create hem, fold 6mm (¼in) to wrong side of skirt bottom edge and press, then fold up another 5cm (2in) and press. Hemstitch. Sew two rows of gathering stitches along top edge of skirt, one 6mm (¼in) from the edge and the second 15mm (⅝in) from the edge. Gently pull threads to gather. With right sides together and matching notches, position along bodice bottom, and sew in place with a 13mm (½in) seam allowance. Remove gathering threads. Tuck under 13 mm (½in) of the lining lower edge to the wrong side and topstitch or stitch in the ditch to the waist. Fold cow face in place, and pin from outside close to where the bodice meets the skirt. Baste close to outer edges.

**16**

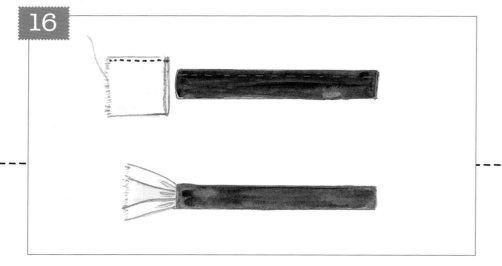

To make the tail, fold tail in half and sew along long edge and across one end. Turn to right side and press. Fold 6mm (¼in) of open edge to inside and press. Pull threads from one long edge of tail tassel to fray. Fold tassel in half; stitch short edges together. Turn right side out and press. Fold outer edges in 13mm (½in) each, and use a gathering stitch to gather top edge. Fit gathered edge of tassel into open end of tail and topstitch through all thicknesses to secure in place.

**17**

On open edges of dress back, fold 6mm (½in) to wrong side and press. Then fold 3cm (1¼in) to wrong side and press. Topstitch in place 2.5cm (1in) from edge to form plackets. Using the pattern as a guide, mark and then sew buttonholes on right placket. Position tail as shown on pattern and topstitch in place close to the top edge. Sew buttons to correspond with buttonholes on left back placket. Sew buttons in position on inside of bodice back to button straps in place.

**Note**
'Fray' means to ravel or become worn at the edge, like a small fringe. You can create this effect with a woven fabric by carefully removing the weft (horizontal) threads from a raw edge. Use a pin and your fingers to gently tease out the bottom thread; repeat the process on the next thread until the fringe is as long as you like.

# Pony Overalls

SIZE: medium

LEVEL: experienced

These overalls are perfect for the horsey set, and they are as comfortable as they are cute. The straps can be adjusted and the cuffs rolled down for longer wear. For a matching shirt, use the pattern for the Elephant Friends shirt, without the elephant appliqués.

## You will need

**Brown pinwale corduroy** – 180cm (2yd) – Cut 2×A, 2×B, 2×C, 2×D

**Cotton print lining** – 90cm (1yd) – Cut 2×I, J

**Red linen** (or similar) for bridle and horseshoe – 22cm (¼yd) – Cut K, L, M

**Peach wool felt** – 20cm by 12.5cm (8in by 5in) scrap – Cut 2×N

**Black wool felt** – 15cm (6in) square scrap – Cut 2×O, 2×P

**Brown linen** (or similar) for pony face – 45cm (½yd) – Cut 2×E, 4×F, G, H

**Thread** to match fabrics and felts

**1.3cm- (½in-) wide elastic** – 45cm (18in) piece – Cut 2×Q

**Buttons** for eyes – 2, 2.5cm (1in) diameter

**Buttons** for straps – 2, 1.8cm (¾in) in diameter

**Fusible fleece** – 22cm (¼yd)

**Paper-backed fusible bonding web** (such as Heat N Bond or Stitch Witchery) – 12.5cm by 25cm (5in by 10in) scrap

**See pattern guide on page 128**

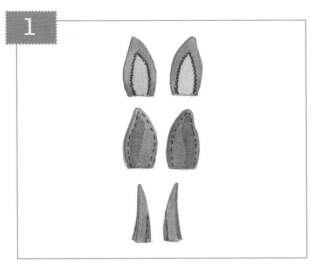

**1**

Place ear centres on ear fronts and zigzag stitch or appliqué in place. Place ear backs over ear fronts with right sides together, and sew together using a 6mm (¼in) seam allowance. Turn to right side and press. Fold ears in half vertically with fronts together and stitch darts, matching notches.

**2**

### Note

Fuse paper-backed double-sided adhesive to fabric for pony halter, horseshoe appliqué, and pony eyes and nostrils, then trace off pattern pieces and cut out. If you are using corduroy for this project, make sure you press it from the back or use a pressing cloth to avoid disrupting the pile.

Cut fusible fleece the same shape as pony face front; fuse to back of face front, following manufacturer's instructions. Peel paper backing from halter straps, nostrils, and eyes and place on pony face front as indicated on pattern. Fuse in place with iron. Zigzag stitch or appliqué in place. Place pony face back on pony face front with right sides together. Sew in place as shown using a 6mm (¼in) seam allowance, leaving open at top. Clip curves, turn to right side, and press.

**3**

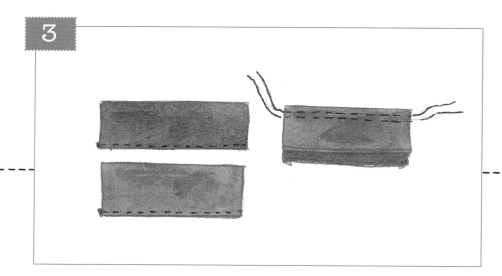

To create forelock, turn 6mm (¼in) to wrong side of one long edge of each of two forelock sections and topstitch 3mm (⅛in) from edge. Fold 6mm (¼in) to wrong side of each side edge and press. Place narrower forelock section on top of wider one, and sew two seams of gathering stitches along top edge, the first 6mm (¼in) from edge and the second 13mm (½in) from edge. Gently pull bobbin threads on each end to gather.

**4**

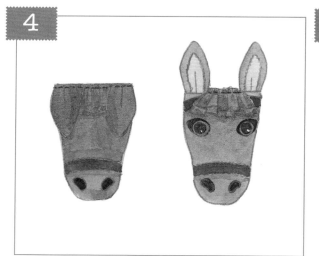

**5**

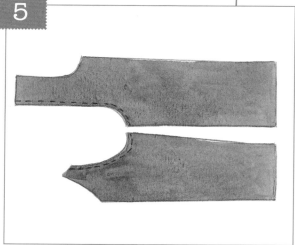

Position forelock between notches on pony face front and baste in place. Position ears on outsides of notches as shown; baste in place. Fold ears up. Place buttons for eyes on eye appliqué shapes and sew in place.

With right sides together, sew centre front seam on overalls side fronts; repeat for centre back seam on overalls side backs. You may wish to stitch again slightly inside the first seam to reinforce. Press seams open.

**6**

Remove paper backing from horseshoe appliqué, position on back of pony overalls, and press in place. Zigzag stitch or appliqué in place.

**7**

Matching notches, position pony face on front of overalls; pin in place. With right sides together, lay overall front facing on top of overall front and sew in place as shown, matching the notches and sandwiching the pony face in between the facing and overalls. Turn to right side and press; topstitch 6mm (¼in) from edge.

**8**

Fold top edge of pockets 6mm (¼in) to wrong side, then fold again to wrong side at notches. Stitch in place 3mm (⅛in) from edge to create a casing for the elastic. Cut two pieces of elastic to length of elastic guide and thread them through the top of each pocket using a loop turner or safety pin. Pin each end in place.

**9**

With right sides of pockets to the right side of the facing, place pockets on overall front facing and sew to facing as shown, keeping overall fronts free. Turn overalls over and topstitch pockets to overall bib front just where they intersect in the front.

**10**

Right sides together, matching notches, sew overall front to back at inseam and outside leg seams. Press open. Right sides together, sew cuffs together at short edges. Press 6mm (¼in) to wrong side on bottom edge of cuffs, pin to each leg opening right sides together; sew. Flip each cuff up at seam; press. Sew cuff upper edges to trouser legs.

**11**

With right sides together, sew long and top edges of straps. Clip corners, turn to right side. Sew straps to back of overalls as shown, matching notches. Cross one strap over the other and topstitch in place, topstitching the straps as well 6mm (¼in) from the edge.

Sew buttons in place as indicated on pattern on inside of overalls bib. Make buttonholes on strap ends.

To keep pony face in place on front of overalls, topstitch in place through all thicknesses (face and overalls bib front) around the pony nostrils with a matching thread. You can also make a matching shirt to wear under the overalls using the Elephant Friends shirt pattern, without the elephant appliqués (see page 36). To make puffed sleeves simply run elastic through the casing created by the sleeve hems.

# Kitty and Mouse Mittens

SIZE: medium
LEVEL: intermediate

Made from wool or cashmere sweaters, these mittens are eco-friendly and quick to make. Look for 100 percent wool or cashmere sweaters with ribbed cuffs in thrift stores, or upcycle your own. Only the sleeves are used for the project. You will need one sweater for the kitties and one for the mice.

## You will need

**Cream colour wool knit sweater** (or similar) –
Cut 2×A, 2×B, 2×C, 4×D

**Grey colour wool knit sweater** (or similar) –
Cut 4×I, 2×J, 2×K

**Pink wool felt scrap** – 12.5cm (5in) square –
Cut 4×E, 2×F, 2×G, 2×H

**Buttons** for eyes – 4, 1.3cm (½in) in diameter

**Yarn** for mouse tails and eyes – 180cm (2yd)

**Thread** to match both wool knits and pink felt

**See pattern guide on page 126**

**Pattern pieces are for the left-hand mitten –
remember to reverse for right-hand mitten**
(To do this, simply turn the pieces over after printing,
and trace any markings through to the opposite side.)

### How to make felt

The felting process tightens the weave of knit
fabrics so that they are thicker and do not
ravel when cut. Place each sweater in an old
white pillowcase and close with a rubber band.
The sweaters will shed during felting, and the
pillowcase will keep the fibers from clogging
your washer or dryer. Put pillowcases in the
washer and run through a wash cycle using
hot water. Remove and put through hot dryer
cycle. The heat is what shrinks the garments
and causes the wool to felt together into a
solid fabric. When you remove them from the
dryer, they should be considerably smaller
and the knit weave no longer visible. If the
weave is still visible, repeat the whole process;
it may take several cycles to achieve felting.
When the sweaters are felted, press flat with
the iron using lots of steam, and cut pattern
pieces as indicated.

Place felt centres on the right side of all four kitty ears
and zigzag or appliqué stitch in place. Repeat with kitty
nose, mouth, and tongue, following placement on
pattern. Zigzag stitch raw edges of ears as well to make
them curl slightly and have more character.

Place button eyes and hand stitch securely in place.
Position and zigzag stitch tiny noses on mice faces. To
make mouse eyes, thread a tapestry needle with yarn.
Make several stitches in place for each eye, and tie off
with a double knot on the wrong side of the fabric.

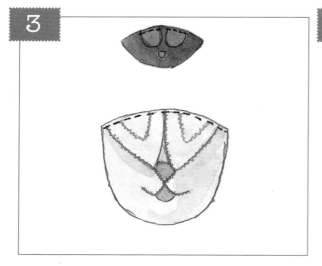

Place ears on faces as shown with right sides together; baste in place with a 6mm (¼in) seam allowance. With right sides together, place cuff side of mitten on top of kitty face and stitch in place on top of basting. You will need to stretch it slightly as you sew to make it fit.

Place lower part of mitten thumb on top of mouse face with right sides together; stitch in place on top of basting. Repeat for second mitten.

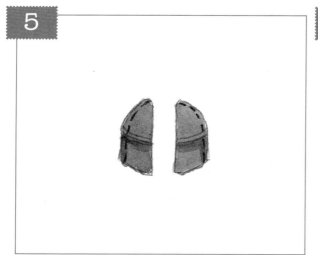

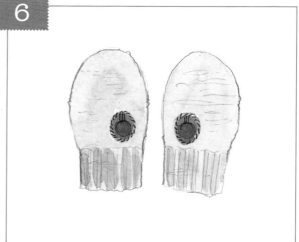

Fold each mouse thumb in half vertically as illustrated and stitch using a scant 3mm (⅛in) seam allowance.

Thread a tapestry needle with yarn that matches the kitty. Position the mouse thumbs on the right side of the mitten palm with the seam down. From the wrong side, whipstitch mouse thumb in place around the thumbhole. Stitch around the opening several times.

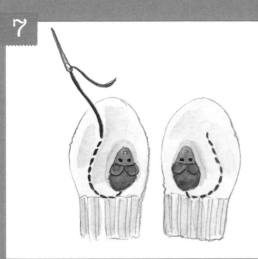

Thread a tapestry needle with the yarn used to make the mouse eyes. Beginning at the base of the thumb, use a backstitch to embroider the mice tails on the palms of the mittens. Backstitch at the end to keep the stitching from raveling.

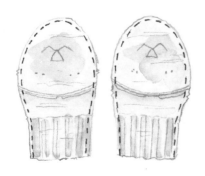

With right sides together, place mitten palms on mitten backs. Taking care to keep the kitty ears free, stitch together using a 6mm (¼in) seam allowance. Turn to right side and try them on your little kitten. Remind them not to lose their mittens!

# Buzzy Bee Rain Cape

Rainy days are delightful when little ones have buzzy bee rain capes to keep them dry! Made from cotton duck, a densely woven fabric which is highly water resistant, this cape is lined in a fun cotton print which adds warmth. Large buttons and an oversized shape make it easy for puddle jumpers to put it on all by themselves.

## You will need

**White cotton duck cloth** – 90cm (1yd) – Cut 2×A, 2×B

**Black cotton duck cloth** – 69cm (¾yd) – Cut C, 2×D, E, F, 2×G, 2×H, I, 2×J, K

**Yellow cotton duck cloth** – 45cm (½yd) – Cut 2×L, 2×M, N, O, 2×P

**Cotton print** for lining – 90cm (1yd) – Cut 2×Q, R, S, 2×T

**Thread** to match all colours of duck cloth

**Buttons** – 5, 2.5cm (1in) in diameter

**See pattern guide on page 126**

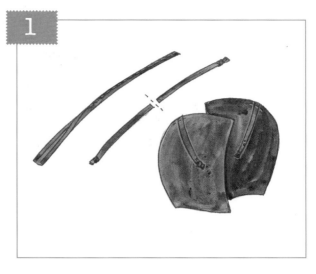

Fold and press 13mm (½in) to the wrong side of both long sides of the antennae. Stitch closed 3mm (⅛in) from the folded edges. Tie a knot at each end, and cut in half to create two separate antennae. Position each antenna on the right side of each hood side at the notch, and baste in place.

With right sides together, sew the hood sides to hood centre. Press seam open. Repeat for hood lining sides and hood lining centre. With right sides together, sew hood visors together along unnotched side with a 6mm (¼in) seam allowance. Turn right side out and press. Position on hood and baste in place.

With right sides together and notches matching, sew hood facing to hood front, securing the visor in place. Then sew lining to hood facing.

**4**

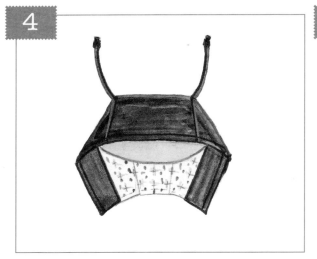

Turn hood to right side, and press front seam flat. Topstitch 13mm (½in) from front edge. Baste hood to hood lining at neck edge.

**5**

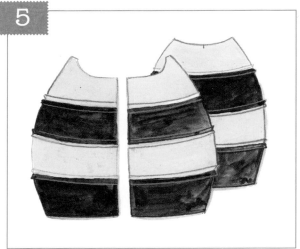

To create stripes: With right sides together, using a 13mm (½in) seam allowance, sew bee body side front sections together and press seams open. Repeat for bee body back sections. Topstitch each section 6mm (¼in) from each seamline, changing thread to match yellow and black sections.

**6**

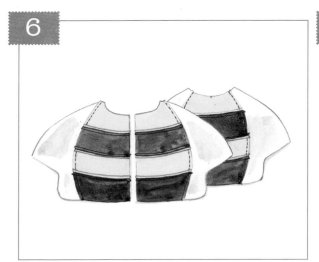

Sew wing fronts to side fronts with a 13mm (½in) seam allowance, and press seams toward wings. Repeat for wing backs and back body.

**7**

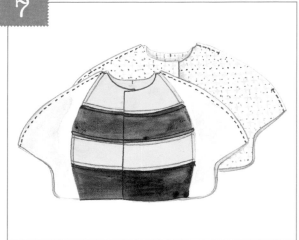

With right sides together, sew cape side fronts to cape back at shoulder seam with a 13mm (½in) seam allowance. Press seams open. With right sides together, sew cape lining side fronts to lining back at shoulder seams with a 13mm (½in) seam allowance, leaving open between notches on left. Press seams open.

8

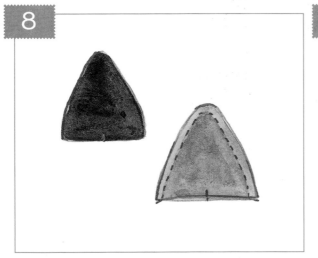

9

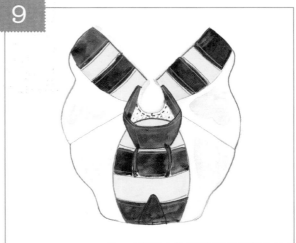

Sew 'stinger' front and back together, trim corner, turn right side out; press. Match notches at centre back bottom of cape; baste stinger in place. Right sides together, match notches of hood centre back neck to cape centre back neck; pin. Pin hood at neck. Sew hood to cape (6mm/¼in seam). Sew again to reinforce.

Right sides together, place cape lining on top of cape and pin, matching shoulder seams and notches. At centre back neck, sew cape lining to cape around the outside edges (6mm/¼in seam allowance). Clip corners of front opening edges; clip curves. Turn to right side through opening in lining. Press lining to inside. With whipstitch, sew opening of lining left shoulder closed.

10

Starting at right front neck edge, topstitch around the cape 6mm (¼in) from edge. Change thread to match each section. Topstitch wing sections above and below buttonhole placement, following pattern. Make three horizontal buttonholes 18mm (¾in) from edge on right side front. Make two diagonal buttonholes on cape outer side fronts. Sew all buttons in place, using placement indicated on pattern.

# Techniques

# Tools of the Trade

To make the projects in this book there are a few pieces of sewing equipment that are essential, as a well as a few handy optional extras.

The most important tool you will need when making your own clothes is a sewing machine. You will need a model that does straight stitching, zigzag stitch and buttonholes, and that has a backstitch feature. Fortunately, these functions are standard on most basic machines. All sewing machines work in more or less the same way, but it's always worth consulting your machine's manual to make sure you are threading it correctly.

There are various accessories for sewing machines that are also useful. A straight-stitch foot is essential, and this should come with your basic machine. You will also need the attachment that allows you to create buttonholes; again, this usually comes as standard with a new sewing machine. A zipper foot can be useful, although none of the projects in this book feature a zipper closure.

Top-of-the-range sewing machines will offer lots of other features but, generally speaking, these are usually decorative stitch options that are not needed in basic dressmaking. You can use the basic zigzag stitch on a conventional sewing machine to finish the raw edges of seams.

## Needles and pins

Although most of the sewing in this book is done with a sewing machine, you will occasionally need to do some hand sewing – this is usually just basting – and so you should have a few needles in your sewing kit. The best are ordinary dressmaking needles (known as 'sharps') in an average size – size 6 or 7 will be ideal.

Another essential will be pins. As you assemble a garment, pins hold the different pieces together before they are sewn. And you will need to pin the pattern to your fabric before cutting out.

Good quality, long dressmaker's pins are the best for the job. The types with coloured ball-like heads are particularly useful since they are easier to see and to pick up.

## Cutting tools

You will also need some cutting tools. Most essential are dressmaker's shears: these special scissors have handles that are angled upward so that the blade can lie flat as you cut through fabric. A pair of embroidery scissors can come in handy for trimming seams and snipping into small corners, and a seam ripper is useful for ripping out any mistakes. Have a pair of ordinary scissors set aside for cutting out paper pattern pieces.

## Measuring and marking

A tape measure is another vital tool. You will need one to take your little ones' measurements and to assist in cutting out the patterns. It's also needed to check seams, hems and other parts of a garment.

And, finally, you should have some marking tools in your sewing box. Whenever you cut a pattern piece out of fabric, you need to transfer information on the pattern to the fabric and you'll need a non-permanent marker to do this. There are various types of marker available. Most common is tailor's chalk, which comes in flat triangles of chalk or in a pencil form.

You can also buy a fade-away marker pen. The marks made with these fade after about 48 hours, so don't use these if you are going to mark up your fabric and then set it aside for a few days.

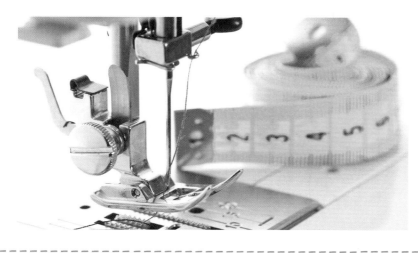

# Using the Patterns

To make the projects in this book you will need to measure the child, choose the right pattern size, and then proceed as you would with any store-bought pattern: laying out the pattern pieces and transferring marks onto the fabric.

## Getting started

The patterns used in this book can be printed out on a standard home or office printer using the CD provided (for more information, see page 111).

Before you begin cutting out your sewing pattern, you need to measure the child you are sewing for to determine what size pattern to cut, and whether any alterations are necessary. This first step ensures that the finished garment will fit comfortably and correctly. Children's pattern sizes correspond to the age of the child – for example, a size 3T should fit a 3-year-old toddler of average size, and a 6 should fit a 6-year-old of average size. However, since each child is different and grows at their own pace, it is best to measure first before you pick up the scissors.

To determine which size to cut, begin by taking the child's chest measurement. Wrap a tape measure all the way around the fullest area of the child's torso (they should be bare-chested or wearing only a thin undershirt), which is usually a few inches below the underarm. Once you have this measurement, compare it to the size chart and select which size to cut.

For best fit, it is also useful to measure the child's arm length and compare it to the pattern to make sure the sleeves are long enough. Keep in mind that children grow quickly! A sleeve that is a bit long will soon fit nicely, and a sleeve that is too short is easy to fix at this early stage. To find the arm length, ask the child to stand with

their arm hanging comfortably at their side. Measure from the point where the top of their arm meets the shoulder – this is the point where the top of the sleeve would sit – to the small bone that protrudes on the wrist. After taking this measurement, you must measure the sleeve pattern piece and compare the results. If the sleeves are too short, adjust by adding extra length.

The last measurement to check is the overall garment length. For a jacket or shirt, measure the centre back length on the child – from the neck bone at the top of their spine down to where you would like for the jacket or shirt to end. Compare this to the centre back length on the pattern piece(s), and make adjustments as necessary. For a skirt, dress or trousers, measure from the child's waist down to where the garment should finish, and compare this to the corresponding pattern piece(s); adjust the pattern if necessary.

A final note: unless the child is extremely tall and slim, most size issues can be corrected by simply going up to the next size pattern.

## Adjusting length

Because pattern pieces are shaped, it's not usually possible to just add a bit on or take a bit off the bottom edge when you want to lengthen or shorten. Instead, it's better to make the adjustment somewhere in the middle of the pattern piece. Just fold your pattern in half widthwise and make your adjustments on this line. If it bisects some important detail of the pattern, such as seam lines, then make the fold a little lower or higher.

To shorten a pattern piece, fold up the amount you want to take off. To lengthen a pattern, cut the pattern in two and add in a piece of paper at the right size. Redraw the side edges of the pattern so that the lines are straight.

### Sizing

Small: 18/24 mo
Medium: 3/4 yrs
Large 5/6 yrs

| Centimeters | S | | M | | L | |
|---|---|---|---|---|---|---|
| Size | 12m | 2T | 3T | 4T | 5 | 6 |
| Chest | 46–51 | 53 | 56 | 59 | 61 | 64 |
| Height | 79 | 87 | 94 | 102 | 109 | 117 |

| Inches | S | | M | | L | |
|---|---|---|---|---|---|---|
| Size | 12m | 2T | 3T | 4T | 5 | 6 |
| Chest | 18–20 | 21 | 22 | 23 | 24 | 25 |
| Height | 31 | 34 | 37 | 40 | 43 | 46 |

## Placing the patterns

The easiest way to cut fabric is in a single layer. Roughly place the pattern pieces on the fabric, starting with the largest pattern pieces (to ensure you get the best use of your fabric). Use a single pin to hold the pieces in rough positions while you check the fabric grain.

## Fabric grain

The most important mark on your sewing pattern pieces is the grain line. This is a long line with an arrowhead at either end. You have to position this line to match the fabric grain before you cut out the piece. If this isn't done properly, the finished garment will not hang correctly.

A woven fabric has two grain lines; the lengthwise and crosswise grains. The lengthwise grain (the warp) runs parallel to the selvedge; the crosswise grain (the weft) runs perpendicular to the selvedge. When you buy a length of cloth, the selvedges are the finished, uncut edges.

If you take a piece of fabric and pull it at a 45° angle to the lengthwise grain, it will feel stretchy – much more stretchy than if you pull it along either the lengthways or crossways grains. This 45° angle is known as the bias and any pattern piece 'cut on the bias' will have

much more stretch to it.

Felt is an exception to this rule; it has no grain, so you may place pattern pieces in any direction to get the most use out of scraps of fabric.

Once you have aligned the pattern pieces with the grain, pin the largest pieces ready to cut. Pin all around the pattern pieces to keep each piece flat on the fabric. Draw around each pattern using your non-permanent marker of choice (see page 102). Use a dashed line

to outline the pattern, as shown in the photograph.

Once you have made the outline, transfer the other pattern marks (see below). After the larger pieces are outlined, add the smaller pattern pieces, ensuring you match the grain as required. Once all the pattern pieces are outlined, and the major pattern marks are transferred, you can start cutting.

Note: it is important to transfer the pattern piece names and grain

## Selvedge help

To position a pattern correctly on the grain, pin one end of the marked grain line to the fabric. Measure down to the selvedge. Position the other end of the grain line so it is the same distance from the selvedge and then pin in place. The marked grain line will be parallel to the selvedge.

lines to the fabric before you cut the pieces, otherwise you will loose track of which piece is which once the paper is removed.

## Pattern marks

Once you've decided on which size pattern you will need and have assembled all the different pieces for your chosen garment (see page 111), you have to transfer some of the marks printed on the pattern onto your fabric. At the edges of the pattern pieces you will notice some small triangles; these marks are called notches and they help you match up the different pieces of a garment as you put it together. For example, you will see notches marked on the top (curved) edge of the sleeve pattern, and notches marked on the armhole edge of the front and back pieces; when you pin the sleeve to the front and back, you simply make sure that the notches on both pieces are lined up.

There are a few ways to mark notches. You can make chalk marks in the right place on the edge of the cut-out fabric pieces; the disadvantage to this is that the marks can be easily rubbed away during handling of the fabric. Or you can cut out a little triangle of fabric in the correct place in the seam allowance; the disadvantage here is that you might make too big a cut. Alternatively, you could use a few basting stitches to mark the position of notches; the problem with this option is that it is hard to be as accurate. Experiment with the methods until you find one that is right for you.

You will also see, on some garments, details such as pleat and dart positions, and pocket placements. Using tailor's chalk or an erasable fabric marker is the best way to mark such features on your fabric. Always transfer any marks to the fabric before you pin and sew the pieces together; you will not be as accurate in

your marking once parts of the garment have been assembled.

Some pattern pieces are symmetrical. These are bisected by a solid line, called the centre fold. You can use the lines to cut fabric on the fold, which is faster (since you only have to pin and cut half the shape). Fold the pattern along the centre fold, and place this folded edge along the folded fabric edge. Be sure to check the grain as usual. Pin the piece through both layers of fabric and check for wrinkles on the reverse. Outline the shape, and cut out the piece, then transfer the remaining marks using the unfolded pattern as a guide.

There will be instances where you have one paper pattern piece but need to use it to cut out two fabric pieces; for example, when you are cutting out the sleeves. Either make two paper pattern pieces, or use the paper pattern to cut out one fabric piece, then re-pin the paper pattern on the fabric to cut out the second piece.

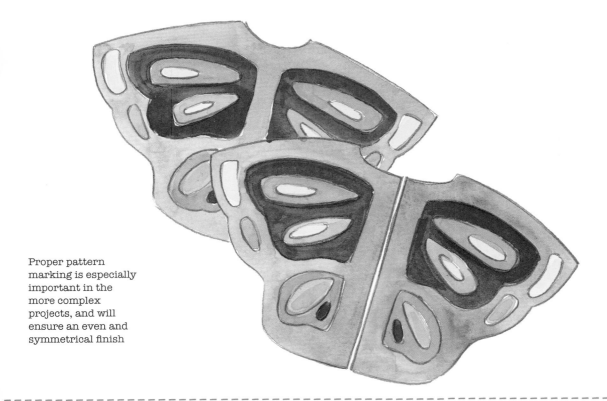

Proper pattern marking is especially important in the more complex projects, and will ensure an even and symmetrical finish

# Seams and Hems

Whenever you sew together pieces of fabric you are creating a seam; whenever you turn up a fabric edge, you are making a hem. These are the fundamentals of garment construction.

To make a seam, you simply bring together two, or maybe more, pieces of fabric and stitch through all the layers. The distance between your line of stitching and the fabric edge is called the seam allowance. Whatever seam allowance is used, it's important to stick to that same allowance throughout – unless otherwise stated – or you will find pattern pieces don't match up. Even a small discrepancy can have a surprising effect.

In this book, seam allowances vary according to each project, so pay close attention to the directions which state the allowance to be used.

### Stitching a seam

When you are going to machine stitch a seam, first raise the sewing-machine foot and the needle. Place the layers of fabric under the foot and lower it to hold the fabric in place.

On the right of your sewing-machine needle you will see measurements marked. Line up your fabric edge to the correct measurement – this will help you maintain an even seam allowance. You may wish to add a piece of tape or a pencil line on the needle plate to highlight commonly used seam allowances.

Position your fabric to start stitching close to the top of the seam. Stitch forward for a short distance and then stop. Depress the reverse switch and stitch backward to the beginning of the seam again. Release the reverse and stitch forward to the end of the seam.

At the end of the seam, depress reverse again and stitch backward and forward for a few stitches. Doing this at the beginning and end of a seam will help secure your thread.

### Corners and curves

If you have to stitch around a corner, machine stitch up to that point and then stop with the needle still in the fabric – you may have to stitch slowly to do this accurately. Lift up the presser foot and pivot the fabric until the continuation of the seam lines up with the guide lines on your sewing machine.

Stitching a curved seam takes a bit of practice. Start by lining up the fabric edge with the appropriate marking on your sewing machine. Then start to stitch very slowly and, as you stitch, turn the fabric so that the raw edge stays level with the guide line.

### Hems

A hem is created when you fold up the raw edge of a piece of fabric so that it is out of sight; when you are instructed to 'turn under' a hem, you have to fold it to the wrong side. If you turn under the fabric once, you create a single hem; if you fold it under twice, then that is a double hem. If you turn under a single hem it is advisable to finish the raw edge of the fabric first by using the zigzag stitch on your sewing machine. When you turn under a double hem then the first turning will be narrower than the second; if the turnings were the same amount, the hem would be too bulky.

To turn under a hem, first turn it up to the given amount (usually 1cm/⅜in) and pin in place. Press all around and then remove the pins.

Turn up the fabric again, to the second given amount and pin again. Hand stitch along the hem on the wrong side using a hem stitch, and keeping the stitching close to the folded edge of the first turning. Many sewing machines have a hem stitch setting; check your manual for instructions if you do not like to hem by hand.

Start and finish your stitching at a seam, if possible, and don't use the reverse stitch function to secure the stitching, as it will be visible on the right side. Instead, when you have finished stitching, pull on one of the loose threads on the wrong side of the hem so that you pull through a loop of stitching from the right side. Insert the tip of a pin in the loop and pull on it until you draw through the end of the thread to the wrong side. Tie the two ends of the thread together several times to secure. Repeat with the other two thread ends. Once you've finished stitching, press the hem again.

### Tricky corners

Occasionally, you may have to turn up a hem that goes around a corner. When this happens, you don't want to leave any untidy edges poking out. Start by folding up the first turning and pressing. Then fold up the second turning and press that, but not at the corners. Unfold the two turnings and trim away any excess fabric at the corner. Refold the first turning, and then refold the second turning, folding the hem into a diagonal line at the corner. Press well and then stitch.

## Finishing seams

As you piece together the different parts of a garment, there are a few simple sewing techniques you can use to help you get a neat and smart finished result. When you create a seam, there will still be what are known as 'raw' edges. These are the cut edges of the fabric at the seam allowance. As a rule, it's a good idea to finish these raw edges in some way to prevent them fraying or unraveling. If you are going to press the seam open, finish each raw edge of a seam allowance; if you are going to press the seam to one side, then finish the raw edges together.

## Edges

The most effective way to finish a seam's edges is to use your machine's zigzag stitch. Zigzag stitch along the seam allowance close to, but not on the edge and then trim off the excess fabric close to the stitching (take care not to cut the threads).

## Trimming seams

Sometimes, especially when sewing together more than two layers of fabric or when sewing around corners, you end up with a bulky seam. To help make a seam lie flat and neatly, it may be necessary to trim the seam allowance in some way. At outer corners, you usually need to snip off the point of the fabric. At inner corners and along curved seams, you should snip into the allowance up to, but not touching, the line of stitching. Occasionally, you may need to trim the width of a seam allowance, especially when adding a facing to a garment. This is usually only necessary if you are using a thick fabric.

## Pressing

Once you have finished the raw edges of a seam, you should press it. Seams are pressed either open or to one side.

To press a seam open, lay the fabric on the ironing board wrong side up and hold the seam open at one end with your fingertips. Run the tip of the iron up the seam to open it up and then press down with the soleplate to flatten the seam.

To press a seam to one side, lay the fabric on the ironing board wrong side up and, with one hand holding the seam allowance down facing the desired direction, iron along it. Turn the fabric to the right side, place a pressing cloth over the seam, and press along it again.

## The importance of pressing

To press effectively, select the correct heat setting on the iron for your chosen fabric. Place the fabric on the ironing board and iron over the element that needs pressing. Apply firm pressure and try not to stretch or pull the fabric as this may distort it. If you are ironing on the right side of the garment, cover it with a pressing cloth first. This is a piece of clean cotton (or any fabric that can take a high heat setting) that protects your fabric during pressing. If you don't use a pressing cloth, you may end up with accidental shiny marks or scorch marks on the project fabric.

## Topstitching

After finishing and pressing a seam you may also want to use topstitching to help make the seam lie flat. This also has the advantage of adding a neat decorative finish to the outside of a garment. Topstitching is simply a line of straight machine stitching that is visible on the right side.

To topstitch a seam that's been pressed open, place the seam in the sewing machine right side up and machine stitch 6–13mm (¼–½in) to the right of the seam, so you are stitching through the top layer of fabric and the seam allowance. Turn the seam around and topstitch along the other side of the seam, keeping to the same distance.

To topstitch a seam that's been pressed to one side, place the fabric in the sewing machine right side up and with the seam allowance to the right. Machine stitch 6–13mm (¼–½in) to the right of the seam, so you are stitching through the top layer of fabric and both the seam allowances.

## Creating neat finishes

Using zigzag stitch gives you the neatest finish to the raw edge of a seam allowance. Topstitching a seam leaves a neat finish on the outside of a garment and helps to ensure a seam lies flat.

## Press as you go

It is essential to press seams as you work, rather than leaving this task until the end of your project. With properly pressed seams it is easier to join together neatly the different parts of a garment. And it's not just seams that need pressing; hems, pleats and darts all benefit from pressing during construction. It's also a good idea to press your pieces of fabric before stitching them together – it will be difficult to get a neat, flat seam otherwise.

# Facings and Interfacings

It's not always possible to use a hem to finish the raw edge of a garment – turning under a curved neckline, for example, might be tricky. This is where you need to use a facing.

When making a garment and sewing together the various pieces, you will need to finish the remaining raw edges in some way. As a rule, the ends of sleeves and the bottom edges of the front and back of a garment are finished with hems. With the neckline and armhole openings (on a sleeveless garment), these edges are usually curved. Because they would be harder to turn up and hem, they are finished with a facing. The front openings on jackets, coats and vests are also finished with a facing, since you need the extra stability this offers. It is also much more effective to make buttonholes in a faced opening.

## The purpose of facing

A facing is a separate piece of fabric that is sewn to the edge of the garment piece and then turned underneath, to the wrong side. The facing is cut to match the shape of the edge to which it is being sewn. On a neckline, for example, the facing will be a curved piece of fabric; the inner curved edge of the facing will exactly match the curved edge of the neckline. Facings must be cut on the same grain (see page 104) as the garment piece to which they are being sewn.

## Interfacing

The addition of interfacing adds further stability. Interfacing is a special fabric that is ironed onto, or sewn, to your facing piece. The iron-on type is known as fusible interfacing, and its ease of use makes it a popular choice. Interfacing comes in a variety of weights; you need to select the weight that best suits your fabric and needs. For the interfaced areas in the garments in this book, a light- to medium-weight interfacing is used. You need to use the pattern pieces shown as 'interfacing' to cut out the interfacing for the corresponding fabric pieces.

## How to sew a facing and interfacing

First cut out your garment pieces from the fabric, including the facing piece. Then use the pattern to cut out your interfacing.

Place the interfacing piece on top of the facing piece, on the wrong side. Carefully place a pressing cloth over the top and iron over the cloth; set the iron to the setting recommended by the interfacing manufacturer.

Once you have fused the interfacing to the facing, transfer any markings from the paper pattern to the wrong side of the facing.

Take the interfaced facing piece and place it on top of the correct garment piece, with the right sides together and making sure the edges and any notches match. Pin in place.

Machine stitch along the relevant edge, taking the recommended seam allowance.

Snip into the seam allowance and any inward corners, and snip off any outer corners. Snip into any strongly curving seams.

Turn the facing to the inside of the piece. If there are any corners, use your little finger or the end of a knitting needle to push the points to the right side. Press.

## Block Fusing

To get a neat finish, you could use a professional dressmaking technique known as block fusing. Cut out a bit of fabric that's roughly big enough for your facing piece, then cut a piece of interfacing about the same size. Fuse the fabric and interfacing together. Position the pattern piece on top of the fused layers, pin, and cut out

# Shaping Techniques

Several projects in this book require gathering or darts to give dimension to construction pieces. Both are described here, along with a method for making simple elasticated waists.

## Gathering

With gathering, the extra fullness in a garment piece is reduced by drawing up the fabric – usually along one edge.

To gather an edge by machine, set the stitch length on your sewing machine to the longest stitch there is. Stitch along the edge 1cm (⅜in) in from the raw edge of the fabric: leave long loose ends of thread at either end of the stitching. Stitch again, just inside the first line of stitching. Wind the loose threads at one end of both lines of stitching around a pin and insert this in the fabric. Pull on the loose threads at the other end of the stitching to draw up the fabric. Adjust the gathers so that the fullness is evenly distributed.

## Darts

Darts are most frequently used in the projects when you need to shape animal ears. Darts take a triangular section out of the fabric – the base of the triangle is at the edge of the fabric with the tip of the triangle pointing toward the fullest part of the ear.

If a garment piece has a dart in it (shown with a V shape), you must transfer the markings for the dart from the paper pattern onto the wrong side of your fabric piece.

Fold the dart so that you bring together the marked lines along the edges; pin.

Stitch along the marked lines, starting at the widest point of the dart, at the fabric edge. Continue stitching to the point of the dart and let the machine run over the end of the fabric; backstitch. Press the dart to one side. If you place a tailor's ham or rolled-up towel under the dart while pressing, you can more effectively press the curve into the fabric.

## Elasticated waists

An elasticated waist is one of the simplest ways to hold a skirt or trousers in place. Since the elastic stretches, the garment can be pulled wide at the waist, and once on it will sit comfortably on the body. Several of the projects in this book, including the Leopard Skirt (page 30) and the Pony Overalls (page 86) use elasticated waistbands. You will need enough elastic to fit comfortably around the waist when slightly stretched, plus a little extra. The elastic then needs to be concealed within a channel, or casing, of fabric.

The simplest way to create a casing is to turn under the fabric and the waistline and stitch this down. Turn under the top edge of the garment at the waist by 1cm (⅜in) and press. Turn under the edge again by the width of the elastic; pin and press. Machine stitch all round the turned edge, close to the fold, leaving a gap of about 10cm (4in). Take your elastic and safety pin one end to the waist at the opening. Then put a safety pin in the other end of the elastic and thread the safety pin through the casing. When the elastic is threaded all the way round the casing, overlap the ends and use one of the safety pins to secure.

Try on the garment to make sure you are happy with the fit. Once you are, machine or hand sew the overlapping ends of the elastic together. Then machine or hand stitch across the opening in the casing.

Gathering

Dart

# Closures

Beautiful fastenings finish a project. Usually one of the last steps, they require a bit of time and planning, but the results are well worth the effort.

### Ties

A narrow length of fabric, tied to another narrow length of fabric, is probably one of the easiest ways to hold a garment in place. Several of the projects in this book – such as the Spring Chicken Bonnet (see page 74) and the Cute Hoot Owl Hat (see page 58) – use ties.

To make a tie, first cut a length of fabric as given in the pattern. Turn under one short end of the fabric strip by 6mm (¼in); press.

Turn under one long edge of the fabric strip by 6mm (¼in); press. Turn under and press the other long edge in the same way. Fold the strip in half lengthwise, wrong sides together, and pin. Topstitch along the short end and down the long turned edges, close to the fold.

### Buttons and buttonholes

This traditional type of closure gives a neat and tidy finish, and helps make a garment look more tailored.

Start by marking the position of the buttonholes as directed by the sewing pattern. The buttonholes are usually made last, so this is one set of markings that you usually transfer to the fabric pieces after the garment has been constructed. If you marked the buttonholes at the beginning of the construction process, the chalk might wear off. To get the right-sized buttonholes, first measure the diameter of your buttons. Then measure the thickness and multiply that by two. Add this figure to the diameter measurement to get the desired length of buttonhole.

Following the instructions in your sewing machine manual, fit the correct foot to your machine and make the first buttonhole. Then go on to make all the rest, making sure that the ends of the buttonholes line up neatly along the garment.

Use a seam ripper to slit the fabric inside the buttonholes. Bring the part of the garment with the buttonholes to overlap the part where you want the buttons. Pin it in place.

Push a chalk marker through the first buttonhole to make a mark on the fabric underneath. Stitch the first button at the marked position. Push the first button through the first buttonhole. Then mark the position of the second buttonhole, as before; stitch the second button in place and push the button through to close the fastening. Continue in this way until all buttons are stitched.

---

### Sewing on a button

Use this technique for sewing on a holed button. Thread your needle with a double strand of thread and secure the thread on the wrong side of the garment, close to where the button will be. Bring the needle and thread through to the right side at the marked button position. Insert the needle in the first hole on the button from the underside, then insert the needle in the second hole from the top side. Take the needle back down through the fabric. Continue to stitch through the holes and fabric until the button feels secure; about six times should do it. Make a knot and cut the thread.

# Printing the Patterns

The patterns in this book are easy to use, just print the size required onto A4 paper. Stick the whole sheet together before you cut out the individual pieces.

Follow the instructions on page 103 to chose the pattern size required. Simply load the CD, open the pattern required and send the document to print. The pattern will automatically print over multiple sheets of paper.

Before you can assemble the pattern, you need to trim the pages. Carefully cut around the edges of the grid, removing the plain white border on each sheet. As a guide, once cut out and joined together, each square on the grid measures 20mm (¾in).

Each sheet is marked with numbers in the corner to indicate the order you need to join them together. For example, there are four sheets with a number '5' in the corner. Join these pieces so that

the four '5' corners are touching.

Use low-tack sticky tape to join the paper pieces. Tape both sides of the joins if preferred. Once all the pages are joined to make a large sheet, cut out the individual pattern pieces. Use the guides on pages 112–128 to keep track of the pattern pieces. You should write the pattern piece name, e.g. 'sleeve lining', on the paper pattern, plus the size used. It is good practice to transfer these notes to the fabric along with your other pattern marks. Seam allowances are included within the pattern pieces, and follow the instructions given with each project.

## Scaling by hand

If you like, you can use the guides on pages 112–128 to draw the pattern pieces by hand (these will scale up to the size indicated by the project). Scaling patterns by hand is simple in concept, but can take a little practice. You will need to buy or make gridded paper with squares measuring 20mm (¾in). Transfer the pattern square by square to the larger paper, using your eye to guide you. It helps to plot individual points first, then connect the dots.

## Pattern Marks

The small triangles along the edges of a pattern are the notches **A**. The notches on one pattern piece are matched to the notches on the pattern piece for an adjoining part of the garment. It's important, therefore, to mark notches accurately so that the parts of the garment fit together.

The most important mark on a pattern is the grain line **B**. This is a long line with an arrowhead at either end. When you cut out the pattern piece from the fabric, this marked line must be

parallel with the fabric grain. Button or buttonhole placement is indicated with an asterisk **C**. A line indicates the angle of the buttonhole.

Some of the pattern pieces have additional lines indicating placement of features such as pockets, appliqués or darts **D**. These types of lines will be referenced in the project instructions (do not cut along these interior lines). Symmetrical pieces also have a centre fold line. For more information, see page 103.

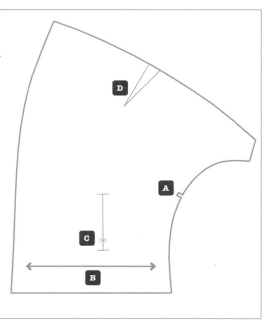

# Roaring Lion Coat

**Yellow wool felt**
A  Ears – 2
B  Tail – 1
C  Sleeve – 2
D  Hood side – 2
E  Hood centre – 1
F  Side back – 2
G  Back yoke – 1
H  Pocket – 4

I  Side front – 2
J  Front hem facing – 2
K  Back hem facing – 1

**Fleece lining**
L  Back lining – 1
M  Side front lining – 2
N  Hood centre lining – 1
O  Hood side lining – 2

**Lining**
P  Sleeve lining – 2

**Cream wool felt**
A  Ears – 2
Q  Muzzle – 1
R  Sleeve facing – 2
S  Hood facing – 1

**Black wool felt**
T  Nose – 1
U  Eyes – 2
V  Claws – 6

**White felt**
W  Teeth – 2

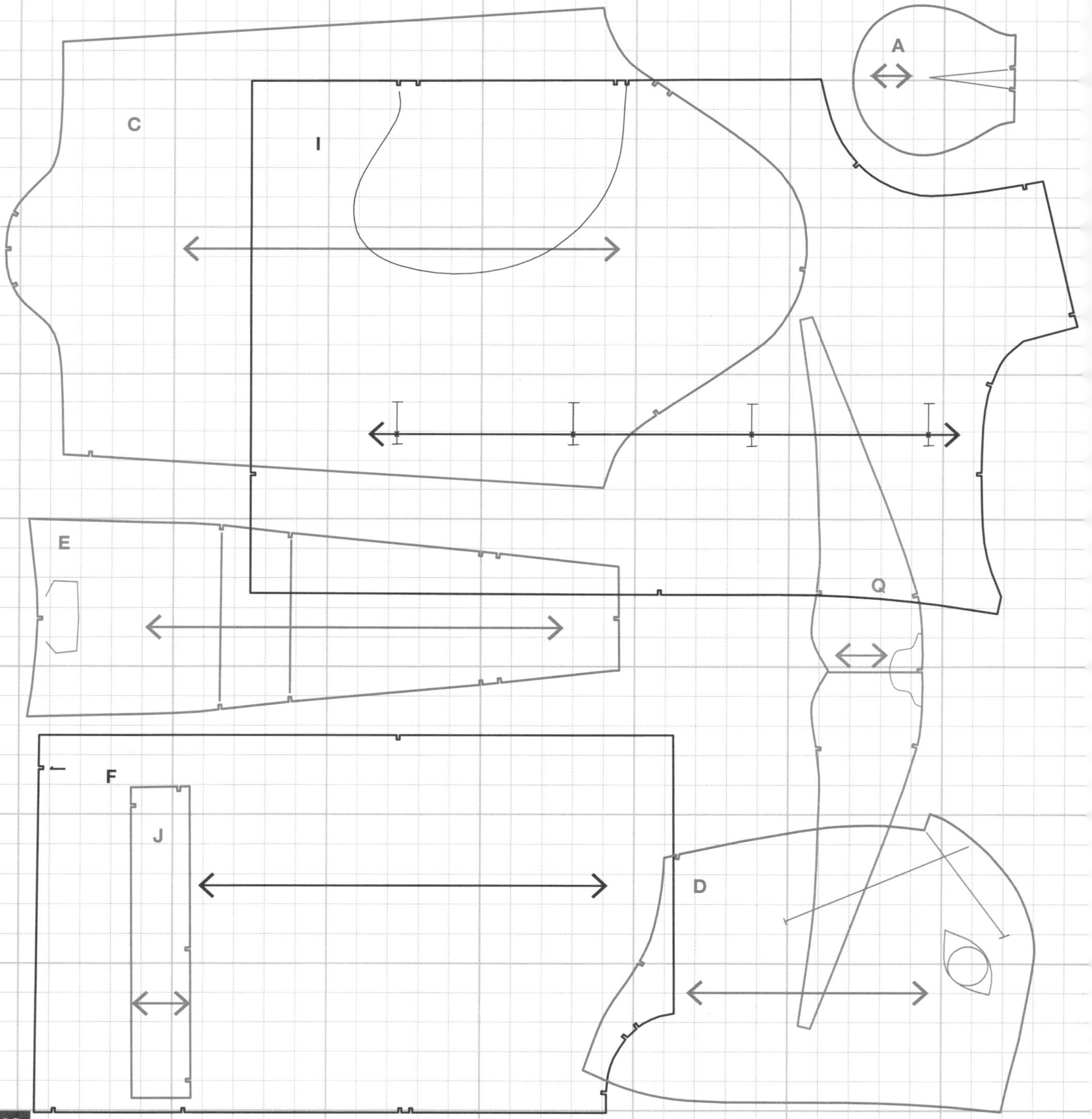

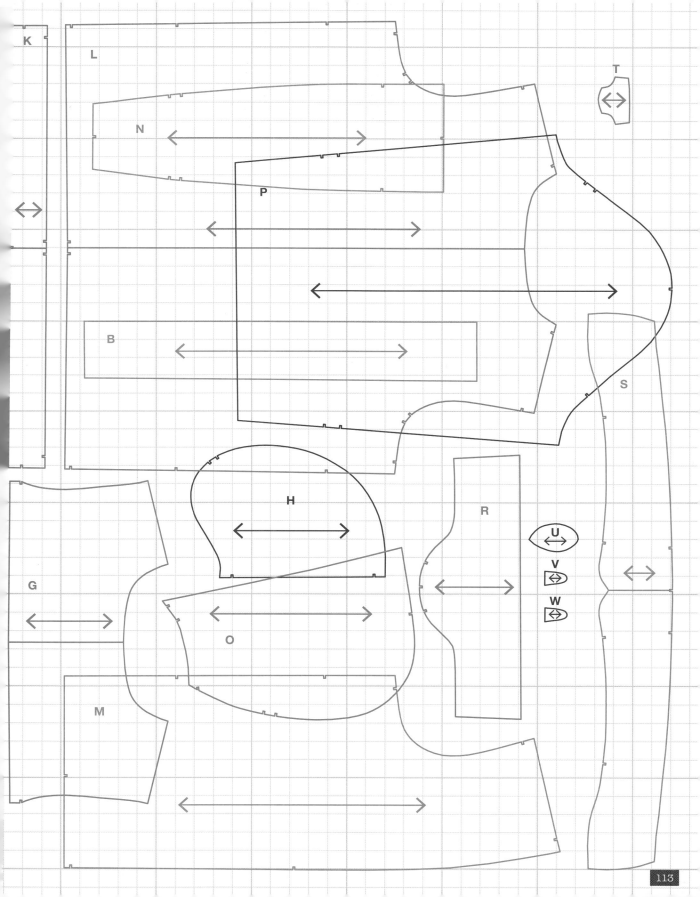

# Bear Hug Vest    Page: 20

**Blue quilted fabric**
A  Side front – 2
B  Back yoke – 1
C  Back – 1
D  Vest pocket – 1

**Black felt**
E  Claws – 12

**Faux fur fabric**
H  Paws – 2
K  Ears – 4
L  Hood bottom
    centre – 1
M  Hood top centre – 1
N  Hood side – 2
O  Tail – 2

**Fleece lining**
F  Back lining – 1
G  Side front lining – 2
H  Paw pocket
    lining – 2
I  Hood side lining – 2
J  Hood centre
    lining – 1

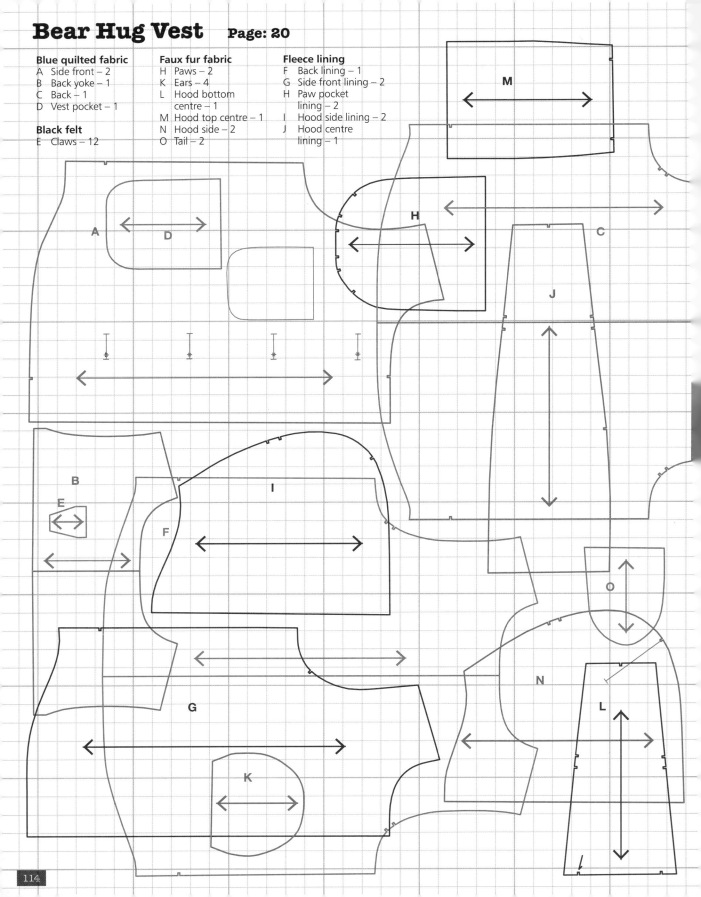

114

# Cosy Koala Hat     Page: 26

**Grey wool felt**
A   Hat side – 2
B   Hat centre – 1
C   Muzzle – 1
D   Ears – 4
E   Facing – 1
F   Chin strap – 1

**White wool felt**
G   Cheeks – 1
H   Ear centres – 2
I   Eye base – 2

**Black wool felt**
J   Nose – 1

**Fleece lining**
K   Hat centre lining – 1
L   Hat side lining – 2

**Fusible fleece**
A   Hat side – 2
B   Hat centre – 1
C   Muzzle – 1

# Little Leopard Skirt     Page: 30

**Velveteen**
A   Skirt front – 1
B   Skirt side
     back – 2
C   Pocket lining – 2
D   Pocket – 1
E   Tail – 2
F   Waistband – 1
G   Face – 1
H   Ears – 2

**Black velveteen**
I   Eyes – 2
J   Nose stripes – 2
K   Mouth – 1

**Pink taffeta**
H   Ears – 2
L   Nose – 1

**Elastic**
M   Elastic strip – 1

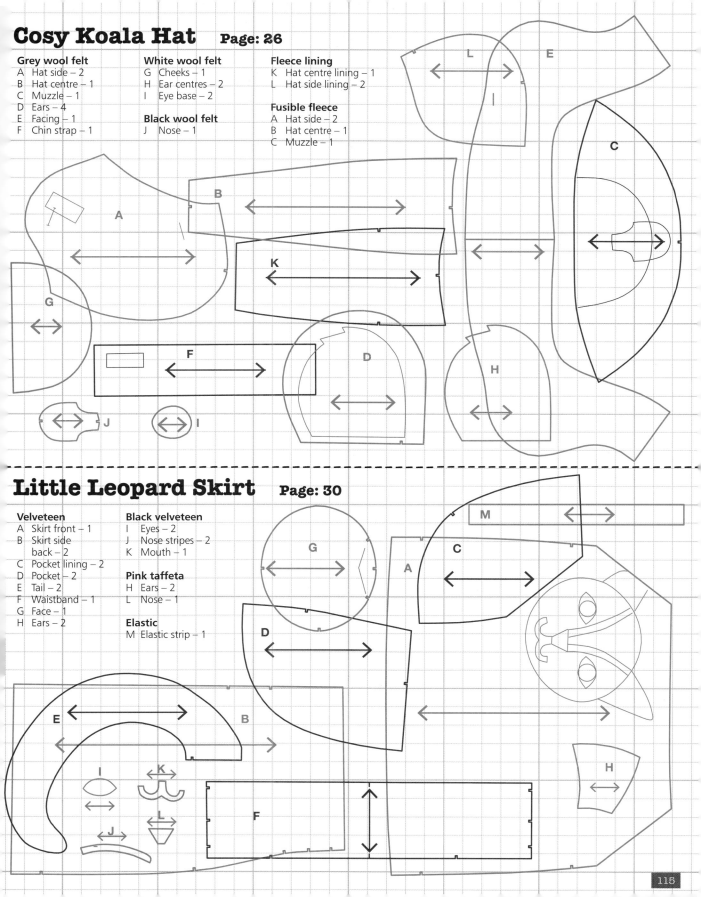

# Bunny Coat    Page: 44

**Wool woven fabric**
A  Ear backs – 2
B  Hood side – 2
C  Hood centre – 1
D  Pocket front – 1
E  Left side front – 1
F  Right side front – 1
G  Sleeve front – 2

H  Sleeve back – 2
I  Ties for closure – 4
J  Coat back – 1

**Cotton print fabric**
K  Ear fronts – 2
L  Hood centre lining – 2
M  Hood side lining – 2

N  Pocket back – 1
O  Sleeve front lining – 2
P  Side front lining – 2
Q  Sleeve back lining – 2
R  Coat back lining – 1

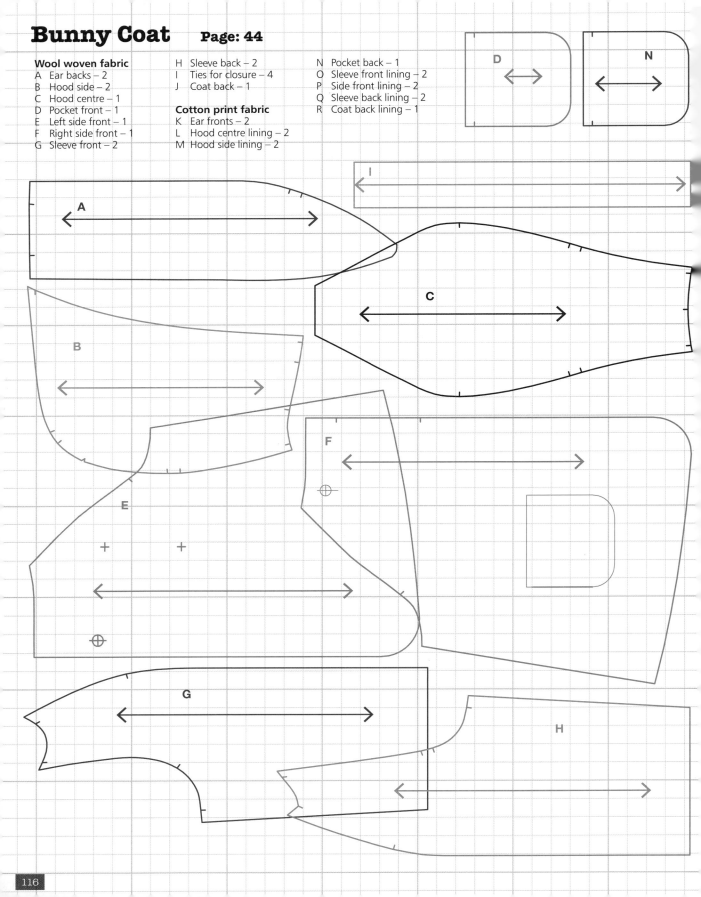

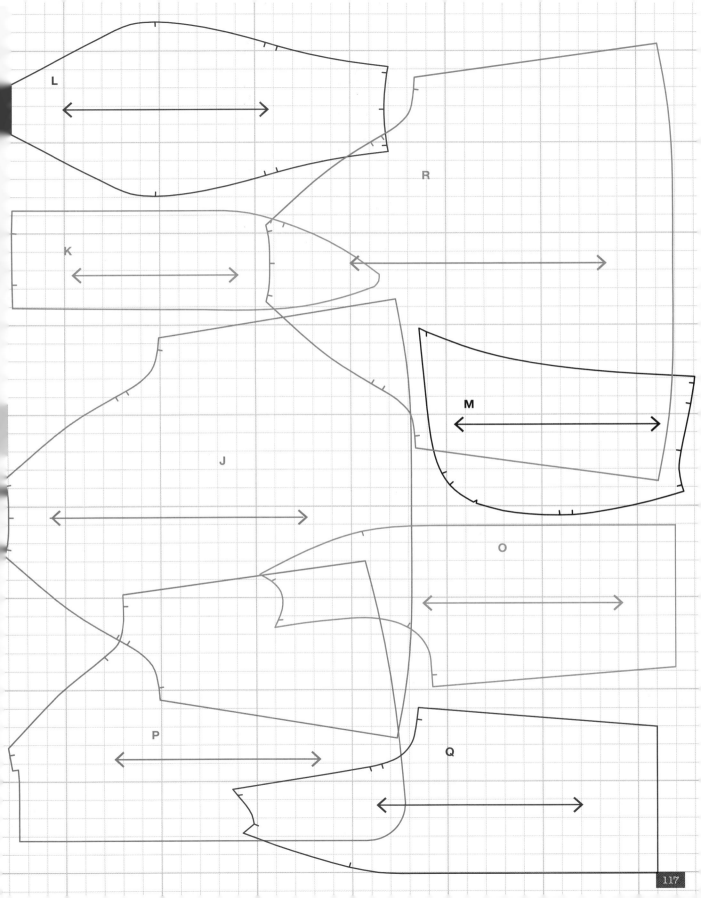

# Raccoon Vest   Page: 50

**Grey tweed fabric**
A   Pocket – 1
B   Hood side – 2
C   Hood centre front – 1
D   Hood centre back – 1
E   Hood facing – 1
F   Back yoke – 1
G   Lower back – 1
H   Side front – 2
I   Ears – 2

**Cream wool felt**
I   Ears – 2
J   Cheeks – 2
K   Raccoon upper mask – 2
L   Eyes – 2

**Black wool felt**
M   Tail – 1
N   Raccoon mask – 2

O   Ear centres – 2
P   Nose – 1

**Fleece lining**
Q   Hood side lining – 2
R   Hood centre lining – 1
S   Back lining – 1
T   Side front lining – 2

**Fusible interfacing**
U   Face – 1

V   Face template – for reference only; no need to cut out

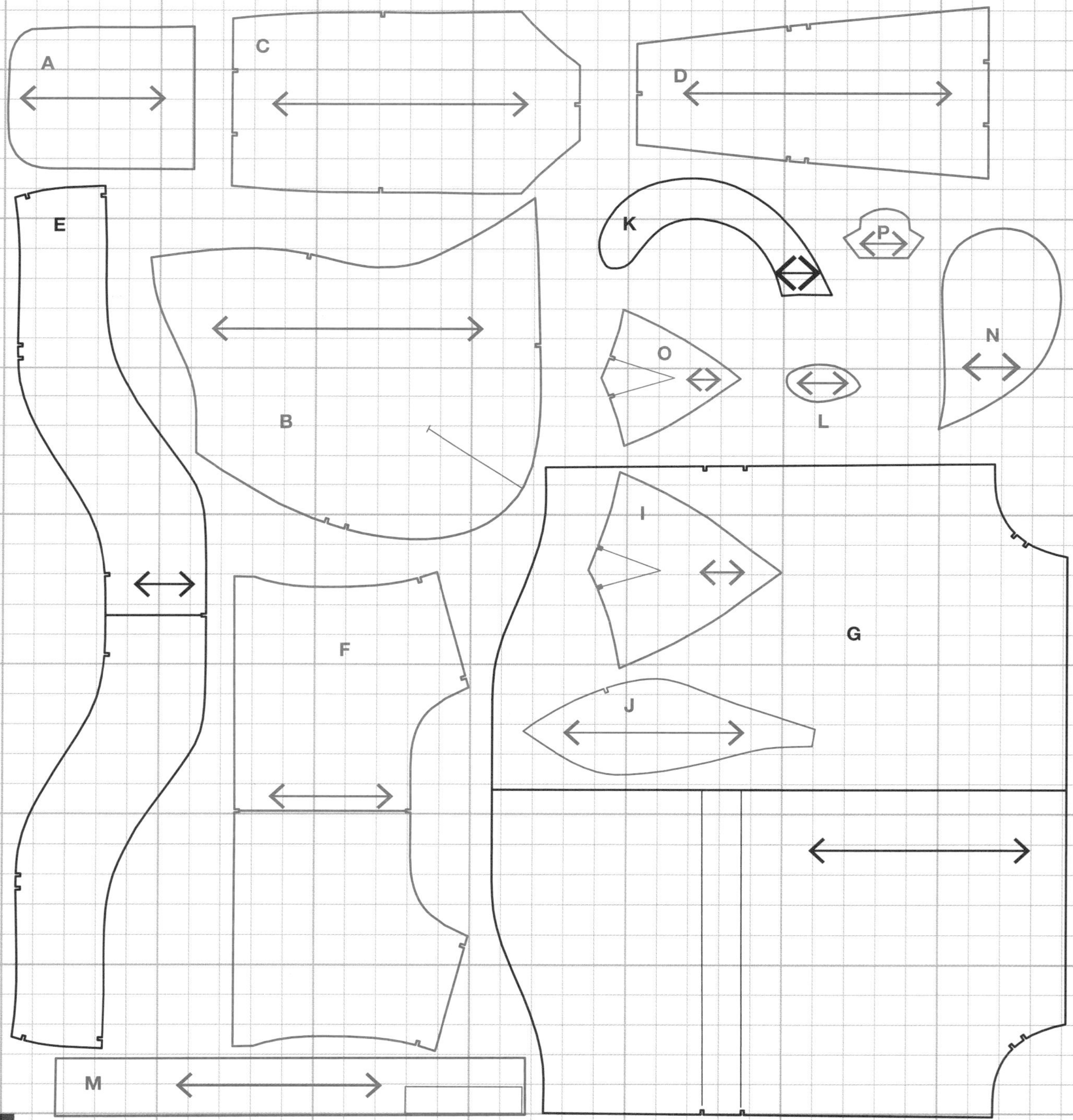

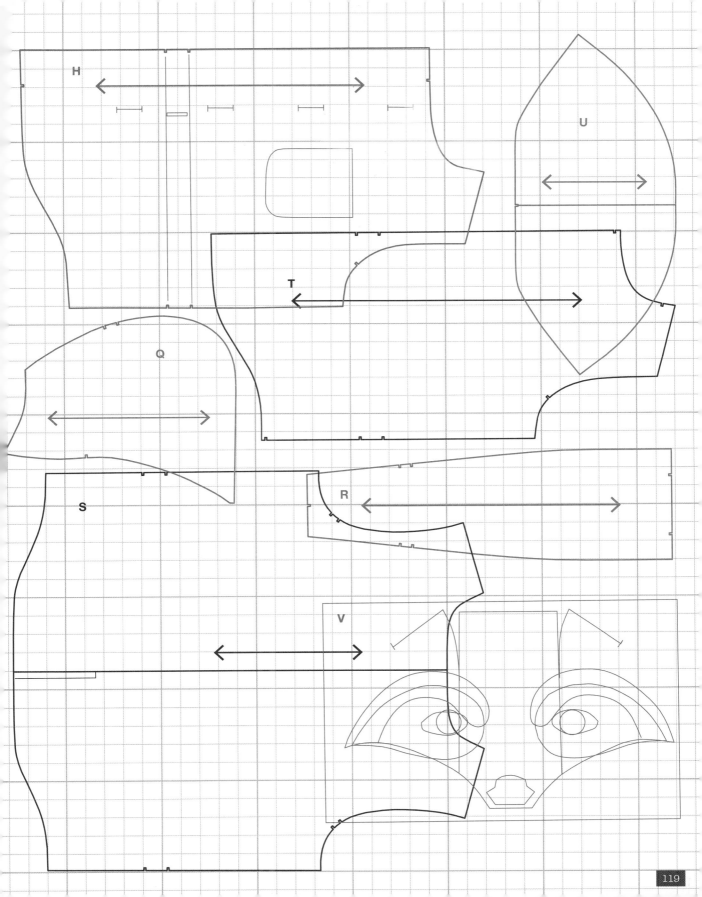

# Elephant Friends Shirt

Page: 36

**Solid cotton fabric**
A  Elephant head – 2
B  Elephant tail – 2
C  Elephant ears – 4

**Cotton print fabric**
D  Back – 1
E  Back yoke – 2
F  Collar – 2
G  Side front – 2
H  Sleeve – 2
I  Front facing – 2

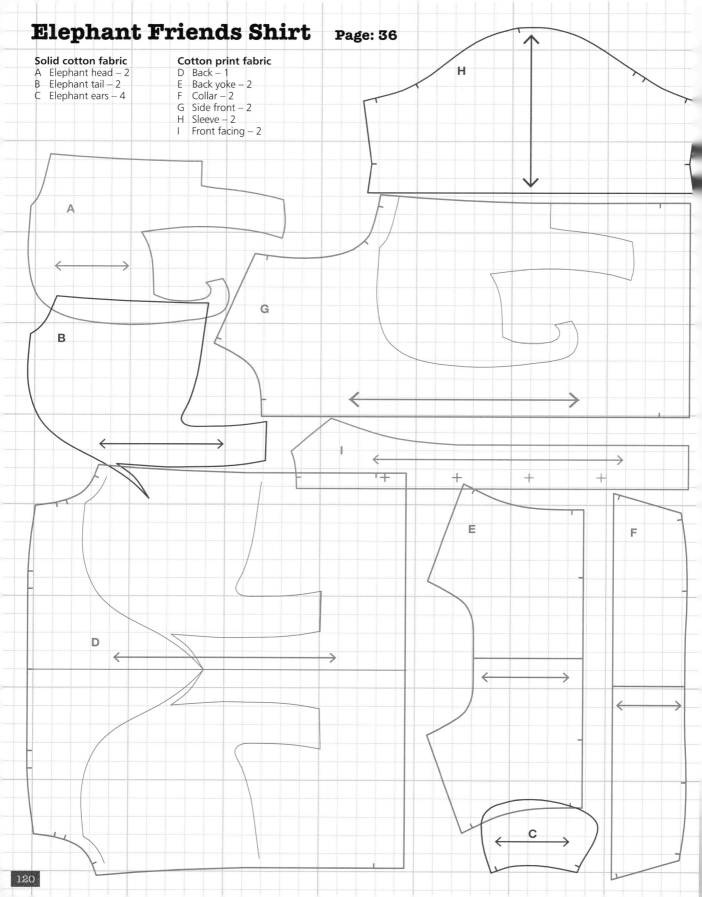

A

B

H

G

I

E

F

D

C

# Cute Hoot Owl Hat    Page: 58

**Pink wool felt**
A   Hat side – 2
B   Hat centre – 1

**Fusible fleece**
A   Hat side – 2
B   Hat centre – 1

**Lining**
C   Hat side lining – 2
D   Hat centre lining – 1

**Peach wool felt**
E   Chin strap – 1
F   Binding – 1
G   Eye circles – 2

H   Tassel strips – 10

**Yellow wool felt**
I   Beak – 1
J   Eyelashes – 2

**Blue wool felt**
K   Eye centres – 2

**Green wool felt**
L   Outer eye base – 2

M   Face template – for
    reference only; no
    need to cut out

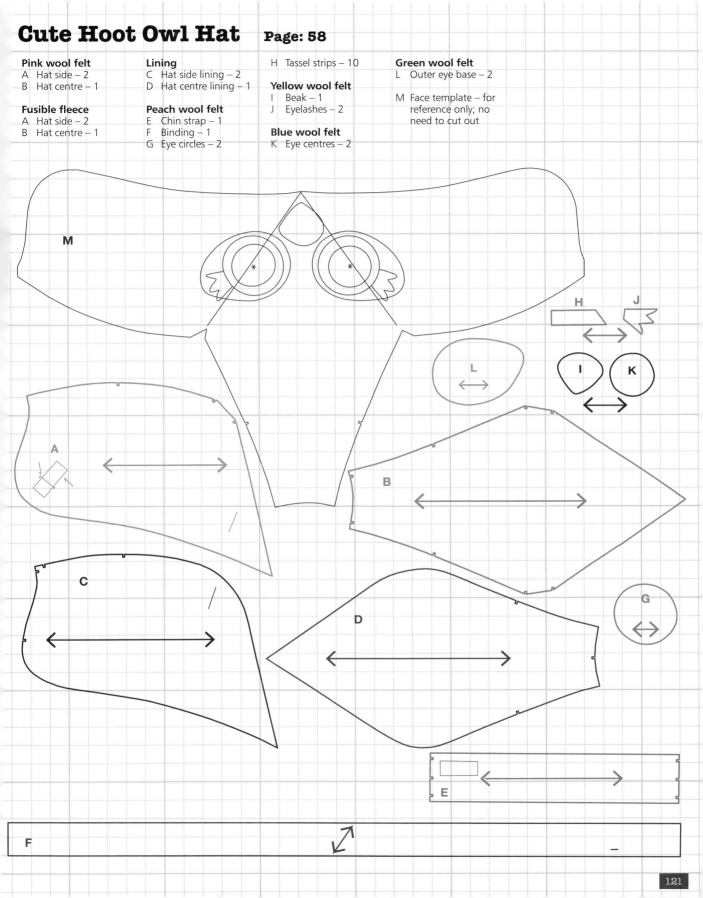

# Foxy Scarf    Page: 62

**Sienna velveteen**
A   Fox body – 1
B   Centre face – 1
C   Ears – 4
D   Tail stem – 1
E   Front paws – 2

**Cream velveteen**
F   Fox belly – 1
G   Hand pocket – 2
H   Cheeks – 2

**Lining**
G   Pocket lining – 2

**Black velveteen**
I   Nose – 1
J   Eyes – 2
K   Ear centres – 2

Dotted wavy lines
indicate long pieces
that must be joined
together

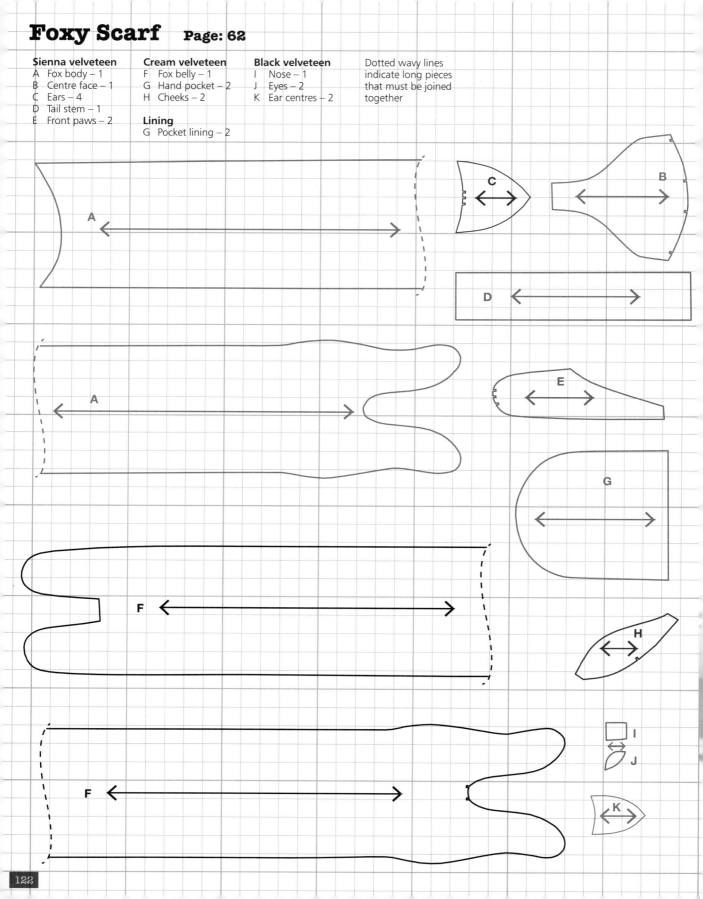

# Little Miss Moo Dress   Page: 78

**White linen**
A  Skirt centre front – 1
B  Skirt side – 2
C  Bodice front – 2
D  Cow face – 1
E  Cow face lining – 1
F  Bodice back lining – 2
G  Bodice back – 2
H  Shoulder strap – 2
I  Tail tassel – 1
J  Sash – 2

**Black linen**
K  Shoulder ruffle – 4
L  Pocket – 2
M  Ears – 2
N  Face side – 2
O  Chin – 2
P  Nostrils – 2
Q  Tail – 1

**Pink linen**
M  Cow ears – 2
R  Cow nose – 1
S  Flower – 2

**Green linen**
T  Flower stem – 2

**Blue linen**
U  Eyes – 2

V  Face template – for reference only; no need to cut

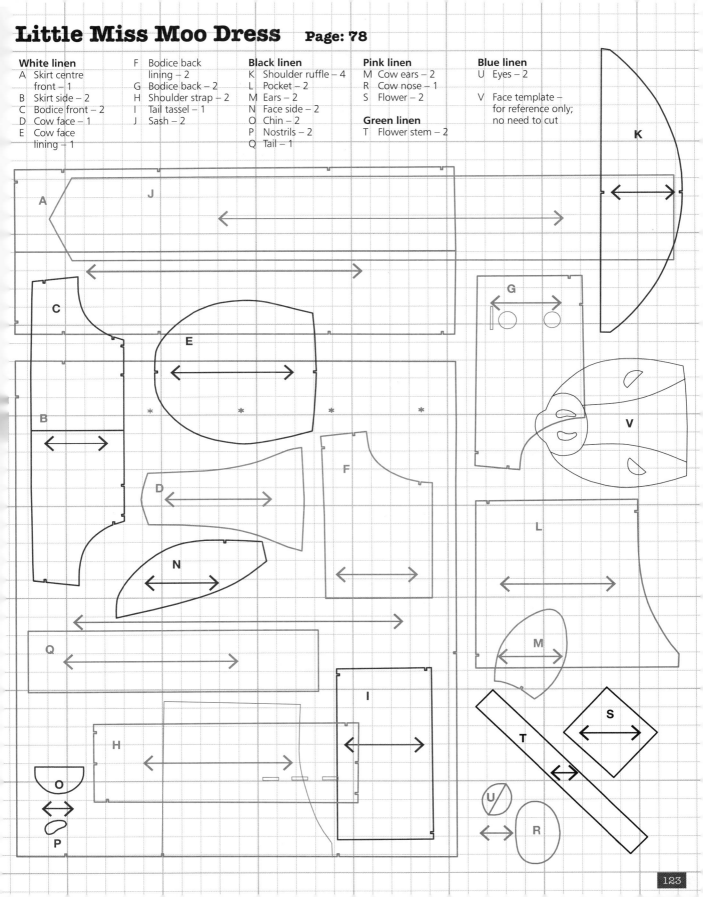

# Butterfly Beach Cape    Page: 68

**Pink terry**
A   Hood centre – 2
B   Hood side – 4
C   Antennae – 1
D   Cape back – 1
E   Cape side front – 2

F   Wing appliqué f – 4
G   Wing appliqué g – 4

**Purple terry**
D   Cape back – 1
E   Cape side front – 2

**Blue terry**
H   Wing appliqué h – 4
I   Wing appliqué i – 4

**Yellow terry**
O   Wing appliqué o – 4
M   Wing appliqué m – 4
N   Wing appliqué n – 4

**Green terry**
L   Wing appliqué l – 4
J   Wing appliqué j – 4
K   Wing appliqué k – 4

Lower case letters indicate
placement of corresponding
appliqué pieces

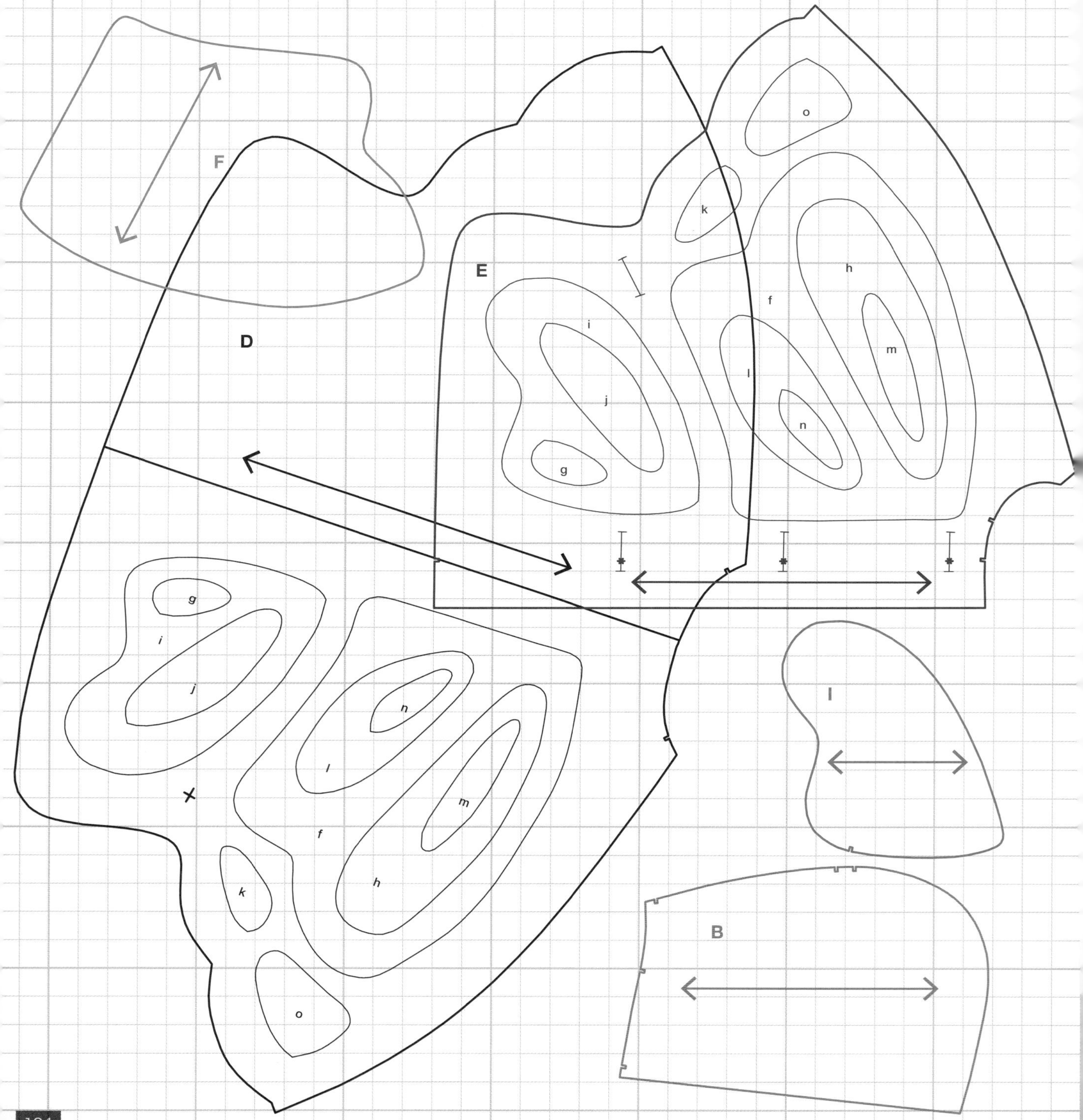

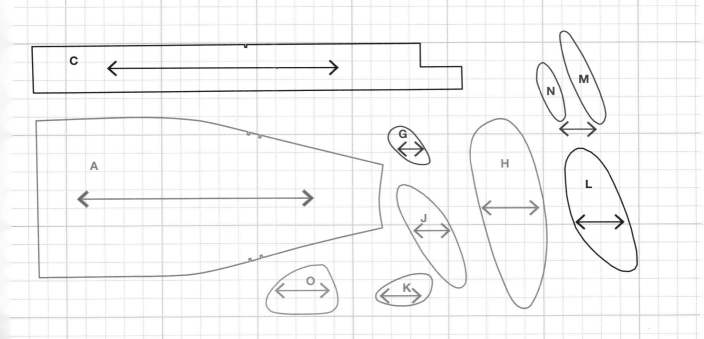

# Spring Chicken Bonnet

**Page: 74**

**White linen:**
A Feather ruffles – 9
B Bonnet centre – 1
C Bonnet side – 2
D front binding and ties – 1
E Face – 1

**Yellow cotton**
C Bonnet side lining – 2
B Bonnet centre lining – 1
F Feet – 4
G Beak – 2

Dotted wavy lines indicate long pieces that must be joined together

# Kitty and Mouse Mittens    Page: 92

**Self-felted knit**
A   Mitten palm – 2
B   Mitten back (face) – 2
C   Mitten lower back – 2
D   Kitty ears – 4

**Pink felt**
E   Kitty ear centres – 4
F   Kitty nose – 2
G   Kitty tongue – 2
H   Mouse nose – 2

**Grey self-felted knit**
I    Mouse ears – 4
J   Thumb base – 2
K   Mouse face – 2

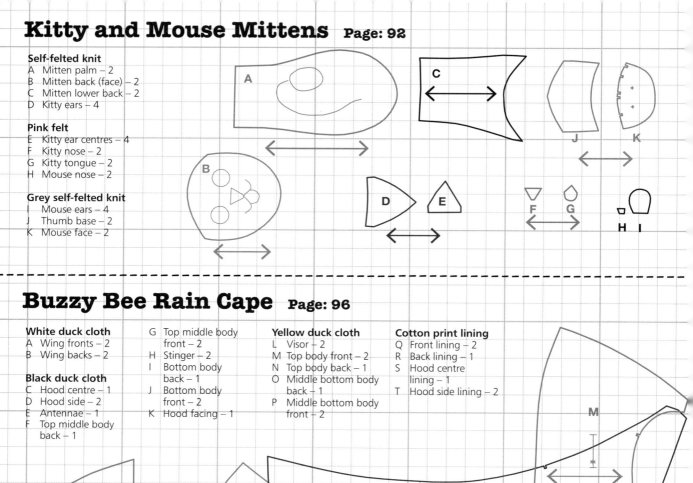

# Buzzy Bee Rain Cape    Page: 96

**White duck cloth**
A   Wing fronts – 2
B   Wing backs – 2

**Black duck cloth**
C   Hood centre – 1
D   Hood side – 2
E   Antennae – 1
F   Top middle body
    back – 1

G   Top middle body
    front – 2
H   Stinger – 2
I    Bottom body
    back – 1
J   Bottom body
    front – 2
K   Hood facing – 1

**Yellow duck cloth**
L   Visor – 2
M   Top body front – 2
N   Top body back – 1
O   Middle bottom body
    back – 1
P   Middle bottom body
    front – 2

**Cotton print lining**
Q   Front lining – 2
R   Back lining – 1
S   Hood centre
    lining – 1
T   Hood side lining – 2

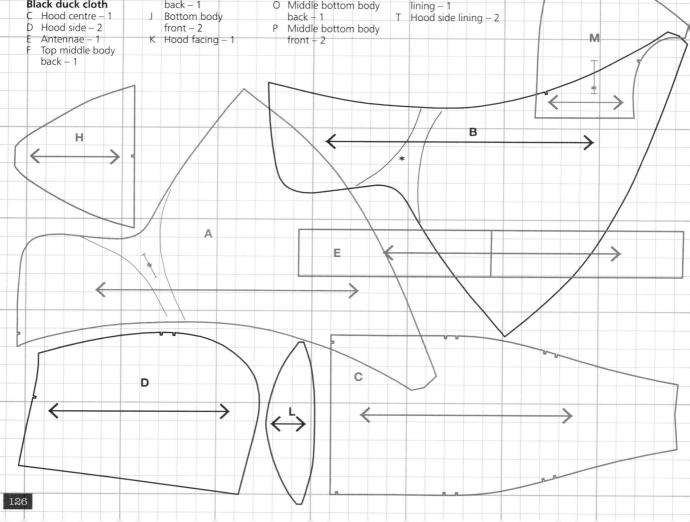

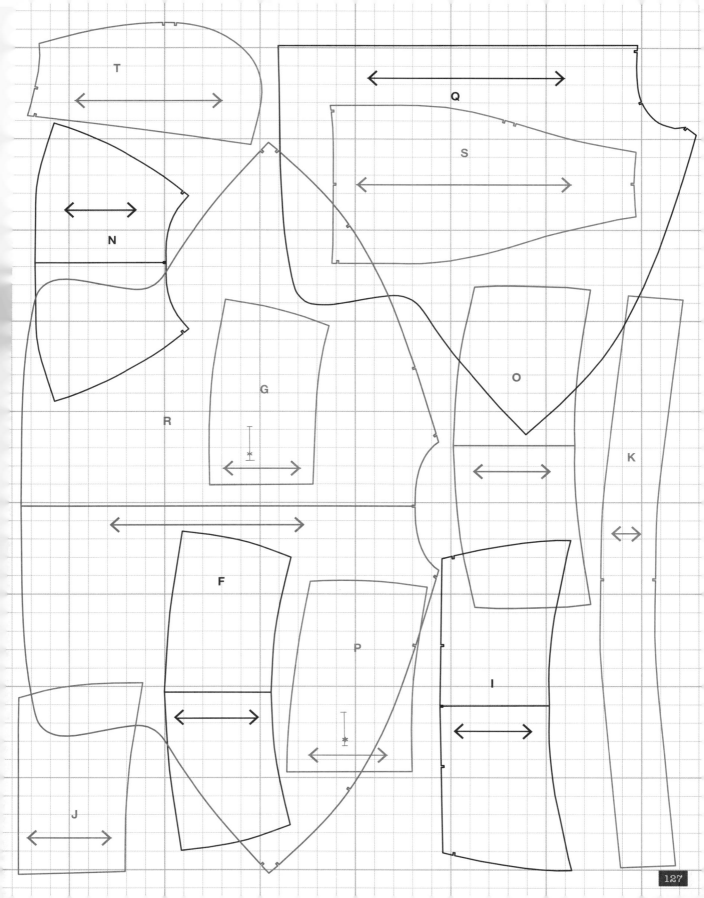

# Pony Overalls

**Page: 86**

**Brown corduroy**
A Overalls side front – 2
B Overalls side back – 2
C Shoulder strap – 2
D Pocket – 2

**Brown linen**
E Pony face – 2
F Ears – 4
G Forelock top layer – 1

H Forelock bottom layer – 1

**Cotton print lining**
I Cuffs – 2
J Front facing – 1

**Red linen**
K Nose band – 1
L Brow band – 1

M Horseshoe – 1

**Pink felt**
N Ear centre – 2

**Black felt**
O Eyes – 2
P Nostrils – 2

**Elastic**
Q Elastic band – 2

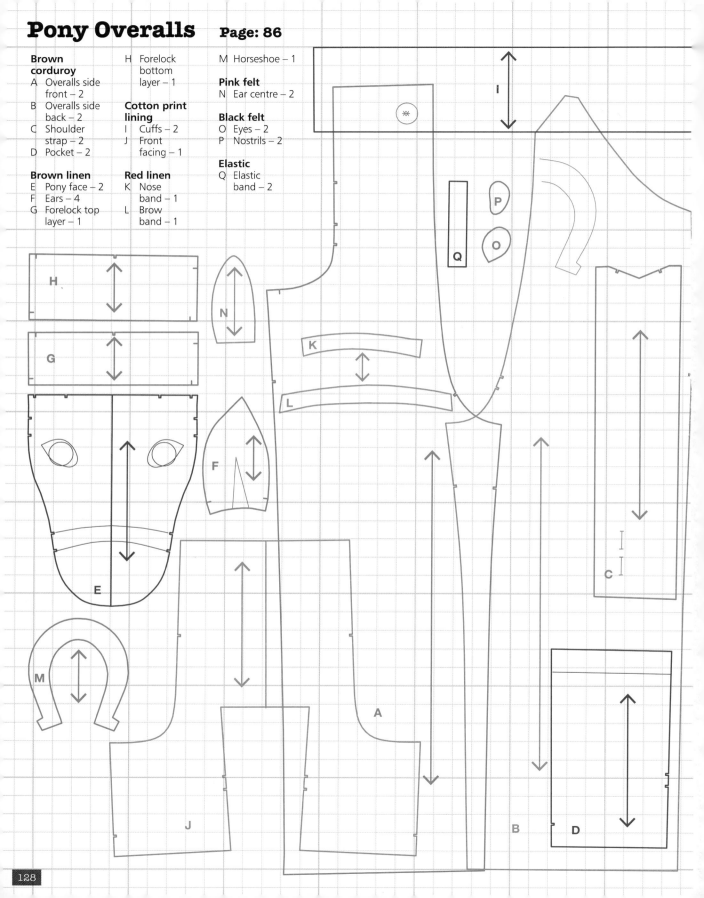